The Bearded Dragon Manual

FROM THE EXPERTS AT
ADVANCED VIVARIUM SYSTEMS®

*Philippe de Vosjoli, Robert Mailloux,
Susan Donoghue, V.M.D., Roger Klingenberg, D.V.M.,
& Jerry Cole*

THE HERPETOCULTURAL LIBRARY®
Advanced Vivarium Systems®
Irvine, California

Amy Fox, *editor*
Nick Clemente, *special consultant*
Suzy Gehrls, *production manager*
Tonya Adams, *operations*
Designed by Kraus & Associates
All photos by Philippe de Vosjoli except where otherwise indicated
Rachel Rice, *indexer*

LCCN: 96-183295
ISBN: 1-882770-59-5

AVS ADVANCED VIVARIUM SYSTEMS™
An Imprint of BowTie Press®
A Division of BowTie, Inc.
3 Burroughs
Irvine, CA 92618
www.avsbooks.com
(877) 4-AVS-BOOK

We want to hear from you. What books would you like to see in the future? Please feel free to write us with any comments on our AVS books.

Printed in Singapore
10 9 8 7 6 5

CONTENTS

A gravid female bearded dragon is arm-waving in response to the black-throated male on her right.

INTRODUCTION

Attractive appearance, moderate size, a naturally tame demeanor, and a high level of personality (by reptilian standards) have made the inland bearded dragon one of the all-time favorite lizard pets. Compared to many other reptiles, bearded dragons are relatively hardy and easy to keep. However, being ectotherms (cold-blooded), they have particular requirements significantly different from more typical pets such as dogs, cats, and birds. We warm-blooded humans don't always have a natural propensity for understanding the care of reptiles. Success at keeping bearded dragons depends on acquiring basic knowledge of their needs, as well as the supplies and technology to care for these beautiful lizards. Providing this essential information was our first objective when we (Philippe de Vosjoli and Robert Mailloux) joined to write this new, updated, and expanded version of *The General Care and Maintenance of Bearded Dragons*.

Interestingly, as we put our heads together, we realized that we had a great deal of useful information that hadn't yet appeared in print but that would improve our understanding of bearded dragons' life stages and in turn ascertain the best way to provide for their husbandry and breeding. Looking at the life stages of bearded dragons also made us aware that, like humans, they undergo changes in growth and behavior, which may require the dedicated owner to make adjustments in husbandry (and general care) to meet the needs of each life stage. As we worked on the project it became clear that there were areas that needed more authoritative and extensive coverage.

As a result, we were fortunate in having several good friends and recognized experts in their fields join us in this writing venture. Our friend Susan Donoghue, V.M.D., a published authority on reptile nutrition who has ongoing research on the effects of diet on bearded dragons, accepted the tasks of writing the section on diet and nutrition, as well as acting as general editor. Roger Klingenberg, D.V.M., another longtime friend who has collaborated with us on a variety of writing projects and who is the author of the best-selling *Understanding Reptiles Parasites,* agreed to write the section on diseases and disorders.

Because we all have an interest in another Australian lizard, the frilled dragon, and because this fantastic species has become more popular in recent years, we contacted our good friend and frilled dragon expert, Jerry Cole, from the UK. He graciously came through in record time with his formula for successfully keeping and breeding this species. Kevin Dunne, owner of Dragon's Den Herpetoculture, also contributed to this work by sharing information on his breeding colony of dragons and providing photographs of his unique morphs.

The entire project has been a rich learning experience for all of us about the value of cooperation among friends. The project also made us realize how much work still needs to be done with these lizards in a wide range of areas, including vivarium design, nutrition, herpetological medicine, and genetics. There are even aspects of basic biology that still need to be studied, such as the contributions of skin morphology and cell dynamics to the appearance of the various color morphs and the hyperxanthic response of certain lines of bearded dragons. There remain critical hurdles that have yet to be cleared, such as identifying the factors that have prevented the long-term captive keeping and breeding of Lawson's dragon and the eastern bearded dragon. These challenges and promises of an ever more exciting future continue to drive us into the peculiar passion called herpetoculture.

CHAPTER 1:

GENERAL INFORMATION

Kinds of Bearded Dragons

Bearded dragon is the common name applied to lizards of the genus *Pogona* in the family Agamidae, several of which display a beardlike extension of the throat when threatened. The bearded dragon most readily available in the pet trade is the inland bearded dragon *(P. vitticeps)*.

Two bearded dragons are commercially bred in small numbers: Lawson's dragon *(P. henrylawsoni)* and the eastern bearded dragon *(P. barbata)*. Lawson's dragon is a smaller and naturally tame species. Unfortunately, it is not as easy to reproduce consistently as the inland bearded dragon is and is not readily available. The large eastern bearded dragon is rarely offered for sale because it also has proven difficult to breed consistently and presents certain problems in long-term husbandry that still need to be resolved. Hybrids between inland bearded dragons and Lawson's dragons are also occasionally offered for sale under the name of Vittikin dragons. Because the inland bearded dragon is by far the most popular, the information presented in this book relates to that species unless mentioned otherwise.

Common Name	Species Name
Inland bearded dragon	*P. vitticeps*
Eastern bearded dragon*	*P. barbata*
Lawson's dragon*	*P. henrylawsoni*

* Hybrids of the eastern bearded dragon and Lawson's dragon are called Vittikin dragons

Inland bearded dragons now come in a variety of morphs including normal brown and tan dragons, German giants, vivid orange-red Sandfire lines, and pale hypomelanistic pastels and Snow/Ghost dragons. Other

This is a very large female bearded dragon. Lizards this size require tanks at least three times their body length.

morphs can be expected to appear in the future as breeders constantly strive to introduce variety into the hobby. Prices of inland bearded dragons vary considerably depending on the age, type, color, and reproductive rate of the morph. You will have to evaluate which of the various kinds of bearded dragons is best suited for your purpose, whether as a pet, a living work of art, or as a source of revenue from breeding.

Is a Bearded Dragon the Right Pet for You?

Most experts correctly rank the bearded dragon as one of the very best reptile pets. These lizards are attractive, active, entertaining, moderately sized, easy to handle, naturally tame (with few exceptions), and relatively easy to keep. Compared to smaller reptiles, they are robust and hardy. Compared to larger reptiles, they are relatively safe for children, although basic hygiene habits such as hand-washing must be practiced.

The only drawback to bearded dragons we've found is

their enclosure requirements. As adults, these space-loving lizards require an enclosure of at least 48 inches long, although 72 inches is preferable. If space is a limitation, a bearded dragon may not be the best pet reptile for you. Because dragons require substantial amounts of food, including live insects, they defecate frequently, so enclosures and substrates have to be cleaned daily. If daily cage cleaning is a drawback for you, consider some of the smaller insect-eating lizards such as leopard geckos. If live insects are a problem, consider some of the skinks (such as blue-tongue skinks) that fare well on foods obtainable at your supermarket, or certain geckos (such as crested geckos) that can be raised primarily on supplemented fruit purees or processed baby foods. However, if you have the space for bearded dragons, you will find that few lizards are more appealing, personable, and entertaining.

Although bearded dragons seem to present less risk of disease transmission than some other reptiles, simple hygiene must be practiced if your home is to be shared with a bearded dragon. Reptiles often carry the *Salmonella* bacterium, which can be shed in their feces and may pose a disease threat to humans, especially infants, toddlers, and those who are immune suppressed. Reptiles should never be allowed on food-handling surfaces such as kitchen counters and dining room tables. Hands should be washed immediately after handling a reptile. Food and water bowls should be washed separately from household dishes. Sound judgment and common sense will keep your dragon a low-risk, valued member of the household.

Habitat

All bearded dragons originated in Australia. Although dragons currently found in the pet trade are many generations removed from their Australian roots, details about their habitat in the wild provide clues to proper husbandry in captivity.

Most bearded dragons live in relatively hot, arid regions of Australia, and thus in captivity require a warm, dry enclosure. However, sources of water (offered in shallow

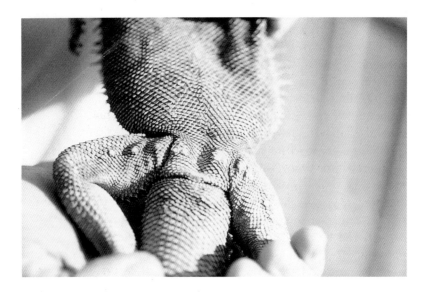

Adult bearded dragons are easy to sex. In addition to larger heads, males have enlarged pre-anal and femoral pores, which are clearly visible in this photograph.

bowls or as fresh greens) and gradients of temperature should always be made available to pet dragons.

Wild bearded dragons in Australia enjoy climbing and basking on rock piles and on the rails and posts of fences. When designing a home for your dragon, include secure rocks and thick branches for its climbing enjoyment. Provide a spotlight so it can bask. In subsequent pages, we'll give you all the information needed for making your dragon feel right at home.

Characteristics of Bearded Dragons

Size
Baby inland bearded dragons are just under 4 inches in length when born. They weigh about 1/10 of an ounce (2 1/2–3 grams). The length of adult dragons is typically 19–23 inches and they weigh at least 3/4 of a pound (250 grams). The German giant morph can reach 26 inches in length.

Longevity
Although there are a few reports of pet inland bearded dragons exceeding ten years of age, most live between five

and eight years if initially healthy and raised under good conditions. We have an unauthenticated report of a twelve-year-old specimen.

Sexing

Although baby bearded dragons can be difficult to sex accurately, adults show secondary sexual characteristics that allow for relatively easy sexual identification.

Accurate determination of the sex of baby bearded dragons is difficult; at best it is an educated guess. Some people make an educated guess on sexual identity by examining and comparing differences in tail taper. The tails of females taper more sharply from the base compared to those of males, which appear just slightly thicker. The differences in tail taper often become more pronounced as bearded dragons grow older. In our experience, this method is most successful when applied to the small percentage of individuals that show greater extremes of tail taper.

A recent technique has improved the probability of sexing small bearded dragons, but it must be performed with extreme care and is best done by an expert dragon handler. This method consists of holding a dragon with one hand and with the other *gently* bending the tail above the body plane. We can't emphasize enough that this is a process that must be performed gently. Careful bending of the tail above the body plane will cause the skin on the ventral (underneath) side of the tail base to be stretched back and show the outlines of hemipenal bulges in males. These bulges run directly caudal (toward the tail) from the vent (cloacal opening). A defined, central post-anal groove is a good indicator of a male. In females slight post-anal bulges may be visible, but they tend to run laterally from the vent midline like the arms of an inverted V. Absolute gentleness and good judgment are required with this procedure so as to prevent injury to the dragon. This method works best with experience and is usually complemented by other concurring observations, such as a wider cloacal openings and thicker tails in males.

One way to sex subadult and adult bearded dragons is to compare the width of cloacal openings. A female *(left)* has a smaller cloacal opening than a male *(right)* has. The photo on the right demonstrates the tail-bending method of sexing.

When sexing subadult and adult bearded dragons you can apply the method of bending the tail as described for sexing babies. As with babies, extreme gentleness is a must when employing this technique.

Subadult and adult animals can also be accurately sexed by pulling back the vent flap and exposing the cloacal opening. In males the cloacal opening is significantly wider and larger than in females. (In baby bearded dragons, this method is ineffective because males need to be older before the greater cloacal width becomes clearly noticeable.)

Many adults are also easy to sex from secondary sexual characteristics. These include thicker tails with less taper in males than in females, and enlarged pre-anal and femoral pores in males. Also, males develop larger and broader heads as well as a dark throat (beard), especially during the breeding season. In adult males, the hemipenes can also be everted by applying pressure with a thumb to the side of the tail base, rolling up toward the vent so as to cause a hemipenis to protrude. This process requires experience to perform properly and is usually not necessary to determine the sex of adults. It is sometimes applied to determine the sex of small bearded dragons but is not recommended because of the risk of injury from crushing

This handler is manually everting the hemipenes of a male bearded dragon.

trauma if not performed with the proper level of experience and sensitivity.

Life Stages

Bearded dragons undergo six life stages. Understanding these life stages is important to successfully raising and maintaining bearded dragons for a long, happy life. The six life stages are delineated here with guides on age and size:

1) *Embryonic/Prebirth* (fifty-five to seventy-five days): In captivity this period of development, which occurs within the confines of the egg, is usually spent in an incubator. However, genetics, diet, health of the mother, and incubation conditions can all play roles in health at this stage. These factors are of concern to breeders and deserve further study by scientists.

2) *Hatchling/Juvenile* (birth to about 8 inches in length): Stage 2 is characterized by ravenous appetite, frequent feeding, rapid growth, and a tendency to mutilate other young dragons, nipping off tail tips, toes, or other low extremities when food is insufficient. We've seen a hungry 6-inch bearded dragon try to eat its lifelong cage mate, which was only 4 inches long. It couldn't swallow the smaller dragon, but it did crush the victim's skull, killing it.

A pair of Lawson's dragons. A female is on the left and a male is on the right. Photo by Patrick Murphy.

Eating and growing are the primary concerns of this stage.

In this stage, dragons frequently perform arm-waving behavior, a type of appeasement and intraspecies identity display. A social hierarchy based on feeding vigor/assertion and growth develops into two levels—the tough, big, and aggressive feeders and the shy, small, "feed after the others" individuals.

3) *Subadult* (8 inches to adult): The primary differences between stages 2 and 3 are size and behavior. Stage 3 begins when the young dragons reach a length of 7 to 8 inches. Mutilation tendencies toward animals in the same size range are reduced. The frequency of arm waving is diminished, especially in males. Growth rate is rapid and a greater percentage of plant matter is eaten. A pattern develops that the bigger a dragon grows, the more it eats, so the more it grows, and so on. Social behaviors are still limited and, if enough food is provided, mostly passive.

4) *Sexual Onset/Young Adult* (12 to 16 inches): Stage 4 lasts through the first three years of breeding. This socially interactive stage is characterized by a greater range of social behaviors triggered by sexual maturity. The onset of sexual social behaviors results in well-defined hierarchies with an alpha male becoming ruler of the roost. Males will perform

courtship, territorial, aggressive, and breeding behaviors. Females perform push-ups to reveal identity. Females also display submissive arm-waving behaviors during breeding. Growth rates at this stage decline because of hormonal changes and the diversion of energy and nutrients away from growth and toward breeding. Adult size is achieved during this stage. After this stage's onset, bearded dragons will normally go through a winter shutdown period annually.

5) *Mature Adult* (fourth year of breeding until six or seven years old): A gradual decrease in reproductive rate and little if any significant growth is associated with this stage of a bearded dragon's life. It lasts two to three years.

6) *Old Age* (usually by six to seven years): This stage is characterized by little or no breeding, at least in females. There is no measurable growth. Eventually, old bearded dragons enter a terminal stage of decreased feeding and increased lethargy that, over weeks or months, lead to death. It is wise to cut back on calories (but not all nutrients) with old dragons and pay special attention to providing adequate levels of water as well as comfortable surroundings and stress-free days.

How Fast Do Bearded Dragons Grow?

In one experiment we raised a group of baby bearded dragons indoors using basking lights (basking sites of 90–95°F) and twist Vita-Lite fluorescent full-spectrum bulbs within 6 inches of the dragons. We offered insects to the dragons three times a day and had a variety of plant matter available all day. Lights were on sixteen hours daily. Hatchlings averaged just under 4 inches in length when the experiment started. After fourteen weeks the largest specimen had reached a total length just over 14 inches. The smallest was 11 inches. As a general guide, under this kind of intensive rearing regimen, growth will average 2 to 2 1/2 inches a month for the first six months, and sexual maturity can be reached as early as five to six months of age. Growth rate begins to taper after about six months.

Our studies show that baby bearded dragons kept

under conservative husbandry conditions can increase in size a mind-boggling 4,000 percent within six months of hatching. Under more intensive conditions, a 5,000 percent increase in weight may occur. A baby inland bearded dragon will weigh about 0.08 ounces (2 1/2 grams) at birth. By six months of age and a length of 12 inches it will weigh about 4 ounces (between 100 and 115 grams—just imagine a human baby growing from 7 pounds to 280 pounds in six months).

What's the lesson to be learned from this? Bearded dragons grow fast, requiring more food than you may have realized and larger enclosures at an earlier age than you may have planned.

The Most Common Health Problems of Bearded Dragons

As with many fast-growing lizards, the most common problem encountered with immature bearded dragons is calcium deficiency associated with soft bones (metabolic bone disease) or twitches and seizures (low blood calcium or hypocalcemia). Calcium deficiency is due to several factors that may occur singly or together: improper vitamin/mineral supplementation, inadequate heat, an inappropriate diet or feeding schedule, and insufficient exposure to an ultraviolet-B (UV-B) light source. Prevention is simple: follow the instructions in this book.

Two other diseases common in bearded dragons of all ages are caused by parasites. One is heavy pinworm infestation, which remains a significant cause of the failure of these lizards to gain or maintain weight. Another more problematical disease is coccidiosis, caused by a type of protozoan parasite. The latter requires diagnosis by a veterinarian and its treatment can be labor intensive and lengthy (see the chapter on diseases).

Older pet dragons may suffer from gout, liver disease, or kidney failure. At the current level of knowledge about these disorders, we suggest that these diseases are more likely to be prevented by assuring proper hydration, adequate thermal gradients, and an appropriate balanced diet.

CHAPTER 2:
SELECTING YOUR DRAGON

P robably nothing is more important for successful keeping of bearded dragons than the initial selection of your animal. You must pay attention and select, to the best of your abilities, an apparently healthy animal to start with. You should also evaluate what you expect from owning a bearded dragon, whether the lizard is meant to be a pet that should interact with you, or a display animal noted for its beauty, or a dragon that will be bred.

Gender and Number of Dragons

Both sexes of bearded dragons make good pets but males grow larger and are considered by some to exhibit more character, personality, and responsiveness. Of course, if you're going to own one bearded dragon, it doesn't take much more work (and can be much more entertaining) to keep a pair of these social creatures.

Complexity of scale structure and color are two of the appealing features of bearded dragons. This is a "normal phase" bearded dragon.

Male eastern bearded dragons develop larger heads than females do.

How many bearded dragons should you get? To answer that question, you need to evaluate your objectives. If you a want a single pet, an individual bearded dragon will fare well enough, although males in particular may display signs of social deprivation by displacing their social behaviors. They may, for example, head bob at you. Because bearded dragons are social creatures, a pair of a male and female, matched so they are close in size, is an ideal combination.

Breeders maintain larger groups, using a ratio of one male to two females. In large walk-in enclosures, you can keep up to two males and four females together. Although adult males will get into territorial and competitive engagements during the breeding season, they are usually not so aggressive as to cause serious harm to each other. Close observation is nonetheless always necessary to evaluate the compatibility of dragons kept in a group.

Baby bearded dragons raised in groups are very competitive and early on will form hierarchies in which the tougher and usually larger animals will intimidate smaller ones, eat most of the food, and grow faster, making them even more intimidating and dominating. If small specimens are not segregated from larger specimens, the small ones will often hide, fare poorly, or eventually become food for their bigger brothers and sisters. Close observation to evaluate the growth, health, and welfare of individual dragons is imperative.

Personality

Bearded dragons vary in personality. Some are more personable and responsive than others are. Some show more signs of intelligence. A very few are spunky from the time they are young, full of attitude, and readily displaying an open mouth in readiness to bite. A few of these spunky lizards can grow into nasty adult dragons, threatening to bite whenever you get near them. In their own way, these aggressive dragons can be an endearing contrast to the typical pet dragon that is tame and placid.

Size

As a general rule, young dragons that are relatively large have less risk of dying than tiny hatchlings. For a first-time owner, a 6–8 inch juvenile that appears in good shape is a better long-term survival prospect than a 4-inch baby and is well worth the extra cost. If good color is important to you, selecting larger individuals well on their way to developing bright colors is the surest way of knowing what you may end up with. Because breeders aim to keep groups consisting of one male to two or three females, excess larger males are commonly available and are ideal choices for those wanting a single pet. Occasionally breeders offer older females at reasonable prices. These dragons are past their reproductive prime but have several good years left as pets and family members.

What to Avoid

Do not pick a dragon that remains on the ground with its eyes closed. After brief periods of activity, sick and weak dragons often close their eyes and resume a sluggish posture. If most dragons in a tank appear unhealthy, do not buy a dragon from that enclosure for there is a good chance that the sick dragons will have infected the few that still appear healthy.

Do not pick a thin dragon with a skinny tail and visible outline of the hipbones. Avoid a dragon with depressions in the back of the head.

Do not select a dragon with fecal smearing around the

vent and base of the tail. There is a good chance it has internal parasites.

Do not pick a runt or baby whose head appears bulbous in the back. It may eventually grow to be normal, but you would be starting off with an undersized or premature pet.

Avoid a baby that shows repetitive opening and closing of the mouth, and makes light popping sounds. These are signs of a respiratory infection. Do not confuse this, however, with normal gaping performed when a dragon is starting to overheat under a basking light.

Finally, do not get the silly notion that you are going to save a poor dragon that is ill or runty. Most sick-looking baby bearded dragons die. If they don't, there is a good chance their owners end up spending quite a bit of money on veterinary bills to take care of their health problems. Nature doesn't select for the weakest and neither should you. If you already have healthy dragons, bringing a sick one home can put them all at risk of contracting a disease.

Signs of a Potentially Healthy Bearded Dragon

Healthy hatchlings may open their mouths and threaten to bite when a large hand approaches them. This is normal behavior for a healthy hatchling.

Look for an animal with rounded body contours and without skeletal outlines visible, particularly along the hipbones and spine. Examine digits and tail to make sure all parts are present.

Select an animal that is bright-eyed and either active or resting comfortably under a spotlight with head and upper body raised. Make sure it is bilaterally symmetrical: both eyes should be the same size, and it should be without a kink or bend in its back.

Once a salesperson removes the bearded dragon from its enclosure, ask to have its belly presented toward you so that you can examine the vent. The anal area should be flush with the body. There should be no brown fecal smears or caking around the vent.

Bearded Dragon Feces as Health Indicators

FAQ: *My bearded dragon has dark stools with a bright white edge. Is this normal?*

Yes. Bearded dragons, like most reptiles, excrete nitrogen in the form of semisolid urates (mostly uric acid), rather than as water-dissolved urea. This allows them to excrete nitrogenous waste while conserving water. Healthy bearded dragons produce dark, formed to semiformed feces with a white urate component.

Runny, pasty, and unusually pale and smelly feces are signs of possible illness, as are unusually large amounts of soft urates. Unpleasant as it may sound, monitoring the state of feces is one way of assessing the health status of your bearded dragon.

Quarantine

Quarantine is unnecessary if you have only the one newly purchased bearded dragon. However, anyone purchasing one or more dragons and wanting to add them to an enclosure with other bearded dragons or to a breeding colony should first quarantine the new lizard(s) individually in a separate enclosure with newspaper substrate for a period of at least sixty days. During that time, carefully monitor the lizard(s), and have a veterinarian perform fecal exam for parasites. Keep a weekly record of a lizard's weight during this period to assess its growth and health. Diseases of special concern are coccidiosis and pinworm infection, both of which can quickly spread in an established collection. You will save yourself a lot of trouble by establishing quarantine procedures before mixing animals.

An outstanding red/gold bearded dragon. Photo by David Travis

CHAPTER 3:

MAKING A HOME FOR YOUR DRAGON

We strongly urge you to keep your bearded dragon within a suitable enclosure. Allowing a dragon to free-roam a room or house may appear at first to be a good thing, but what may be perceived as freedom for the lizard can become a death trap. Dragons that are loose in households fail to keep themselves adequately warm and hydrated. They can become immune-suppressed, falling ill from infections. Moreover, loose dragons may be stepped on by humans and preyed upon by household dogs and cats. They may receive serious or fatal electrical shocks from wires or equally serious trauma from toppling books, lamps, and the like. Loose dragons risk setting households on fire by bringing combustibles such as curtains into contact with hot items such as lightbulbs. Responsible bearded dragon owners who are dedicated to providing the best for their pets keep their dragons in appropriate enclosures and let them out only when they can be supervised closely.

Enclosures

Bearded dragons are moderate-sized lizards that, as they grow, require large enclosures. When deciding on enclosures, it is important to consider the bearded dragon as a two-stage lizard even if you want to invest right away in the larger enclosure it will need when fully grown. You can start a baby for the first four to six months in a 30-inch-long enclosure. Keeping a baby dragon in a larger enclosure can be problematic, because the dragon may fail to find its food, water, basking sites, and shelters. As the baby

Above: Large, molded plastic snake cages with sliding glass fronts can be modified to accommodate bearded dragons. This is a cage produced by Bush Herpetological that was designed to house desert iguanas, a species with requirements similar to bearded dragons. With plastic enclosures, take care in placing the spotlights to avoid melting the plastic. Photo by Val Brinkerhoff, courtesy of Dan McCarron

Left: This 30-inch vivarium with front sliding-glass doors is set up for temporary display of baby bearded dragons. Snake plants and a pony-tailed palm decorate the display.

grows, however, you will need to provide a larger enclosure.

The smallest enclosure for one or two adult bearded dragons is either a 4-foot x 2-foot vivarium or a 6-foot x 18-inch vivarium. At the very limits, a standard 55-gallon (48-inch x 13- inch) vivarium houses a single adult specimen. Anything smaller will restrict activity in a way that is not optimal for the animal's welfare. Enclosure size requirements need to be considered before you decide to purchase one of these lizards.

The most widely sold enclosures in the reptile trade are all-glass tanks with sliding screen tops. These are fine for bearded dragons except for two problems: many stores do

In this outdoor breeding setup, wooden pallets are joined to create sites for perching and basking as well as shade.

not carry the larger sizes; and transportation and weight of these enclosures may become an issue. There are large, lightweight plastic molded enclosures with sliding glass fronts sold in the reptile trade (e.g., Bush Herpetological and Vision Herpetological) that can be designed for housing bearded dragons. These enclosures can be mailordered if your local reptile store does not stock them.

Outdoor Enclosures

In a few warm areas of the United States, such as southern California, bearded dragons can be kept in outdoor screened or covered pens year-round as long as they are provided with shelters from rain and have areas of soil or piles of hay to burrow into. Breeders have built effective pens inside greenhouses. Greenhouses should have controls for monitoring and maintaining desired temperatures including whitewash, opening panels, fans, and heaters.

In most other areas of the U.S., bearded dragons can be kept outdoors in simple pens during warm months. Make sure you build secure enclosures with screen or mesh tops to prevent escape and to keep out potential predators such as foxes, raccoons, cats, and birds of prey. Inexpensive alternatives to pens are large plastic screen enclosures now sold in the reptile trade. They are ideal for allowing lizards to bask outdoors in sunlight (see the chapter on heating and lighting). It is important not to place these all-screen enclosures on concrete or asphalt. Because both of these surfaces absorb heat when exposed to sun, dragons may overheat and die if housed in a screen cage without shade, water, and climbing areas.

Substrates

Because of the potential risks of sand impaction, many people choose to initially raise baby bearded dragons on newspaper. For animals over 8 inches, we use silica-based, dust-free play sand (used in children's sandboxes) as a substrate and have never had problems with impaction. Our evaluations of various substrates are as follows:

❑ *No Substrate*: Many breeders raise their babies on bare floors within plastic tubs or glass tanks. Advantages of bare floors include easy monitoring of stools, lack of hiding places for crickets, minimal risk of impaction, and less-intensive maintenance. Bare floor enclosures are easy to empty of landscape structures and can be moved outside for washing with a garden hose. A disadvantage is that the floors require regular wiping. As the dragon grows larger and messier, bare tanks become unattractive and tedious to clean. With larger animals, the hard, smooth floor surface can also lead to overgrown nails and bent toes.

❑ *Newspaper:* This is the substrate most recommended for quarantine and treatment of sick animals. Newspaper is cheap, readily available, easy to replace, and well suited for examining feces. Many specialists recommend newspaper for initially raising babies because it allows monitoring of stools and eliminates any risks of impaction. Downsides are that newspaper is visually unattractive, and regular or daily replacement can be labor intensive. If used with adult dragons on a long-term basis, there is a risk of overgrown nails and bent toes.

❑ *Sand:* Sand is our favorite substrate. We have never had problems using a variety of sands with bearded dragons of all ages (yes, we use sand with babies), but there are reports of sand impaction in babies. For this reason, we recommend paper towels, newspaper, or brown butcher paper for hatchlings up to a length of 8 inches. After that size, sand is the most natural-looking and easy-to-maintain substrate for bearded dragons. We use play sand because it is relatively dust-free. There are other types of sand, including limestone sand, sold in the reptile trade that are attractive and may work with bearded dragons. However, we're concerned about reports of baby dragons becoming seriously ill from intestinal impactions following the ingestion of sands containing calcium. Until more information becomes available, they are probably best used only with larger bearded dragons. Avoid unscreened/unwashed sands, particularly unprocessed silica sands because of health risks from inhaling dust lifted by the dragons' digging. To clean fecal material, remove fouled sections of sand daily using a scoop. Change sand every four weeks or as needed.

❏ *Sandy Soil:* Mixes of sand and soil work well with bearded dragons. A problem with soil is that it can make dragon colors appear more brown and less colorful over time. Dust is also a problem. As with substrates of just sand, spot cleaning is easy. Sandy soil must be replaced on a regular basis. In outdoor setups, natural soils make up the floor of most screenhouses and greenhouses and generally work well with bearded dragons.

❏ *Alfalfa Pellets and Rabbit Pellets:* Alfalfa pellets are absorbent but have drawbacks. Some people develop serious allergies to alfalfa. Moreover, the pellets exude a strong odor when wet and can crumble, turning into a pervasive dust that escapes enclosures. There is also a risk of flour beetle infestation. These beetles are harmless but can spread and infest any grain-based food in your kitchen. (In time, you could have hundreds of tiny beetles scattered throughout your house). Alfalfa is too soft a substrate for adequate nail wear. Some veterinari-

ans believe that there is a higher incidence of respiratory disease in lizards housed on alfalfa pellets and rabbit pellets. These pellets are quick to mold when they become wet, so lizards may inhale mold spores, predisposing them to respiratory disease. Clearly, these pellets are not our favorite substrate.

This 36-inch vivarium has been designed for housing baby bearded dragons. It includes perching areas, live plants, a basking light, a UV-B fluorescent bulb, and a hot rock as a secondary heat source.

Landscaping

Many new owners make the understandable error of landscaping their bearded dragon vivaria without any climbing areas. Not only does this limit the space available for your dragon's activity but also makes for a dull display. Remember, inland bearded dragons are semi-arboreal and like to climb on rocks and dried wood. In Australia, they are often seen on the top of fence posts and rails. These perching sites can be reproduced in captivity by adding large sections of dried grape wood, fig wood, cork bark rounds, or rocks. Ledges along the back and sides of a tank can also be created. These raised areas make ideal basking sites and most hobbyists design them so that they are located under spotlights. At least one raised site should be provided per enclosure. In addition to a raised area, you should also have plenty of open ground, maintaining at least two-thirds of the floor surface as open space. Bearded

In this custom indoor display, stacked rocks serve as basking site and shelter. The plant is a *Dracaena marginata*, a species readily available in stores that sell houseplants. Photo by Val Brinkerhoff.

dragons also enjoy shelters for sleeping at night or for brumation (shutting down) during the winter rest or period. Our favorite shelters for bearded dragons are big slabs of rounded cork bark. They're attractive, light, and easy to clean.

Nail Wear

In captivity, if lizards are kept on solid surfaces or on soft substrates they can end up with overgrown nails and digits that bend to the side. To prevent this, consider scattering rough pebbles on the substrate surface or adding flat sections of rough rock such as limestone to the landscape design. Lizards wear down nails by running or climbing on rock surfaces.

Plants for Bearded Dragon Setups

We have received many letters requesting lists of plants that are well suited for bearded dragon setups. We know that popular vivarium plants such as pothos or Chinese evergreen are quickly crushed, nipped, trashed, and dried up in a bearded dragon setup. Only a few species of plants are tough enough to hold up to bearded dragon abuse indoors. Our top choices include ponytail palms (*Beaucarnea recurvata*) and snake plants (*Sansevieria* spp.), particularly the tougher ones with thick or cylindrical leaves that are more adapted to arid conditions. With

These bearded dragons in an outdoor enclosure particularly like to perch on large jade plants.

smaller dragons, jade plants *(Crassula argentea)* fare reasonably well but do not usually grow thick and strong enough indoors to withstand the weight of larger dragons. The only cactus we recommend is the spineless tree opuntia *(Consolea falcata)*. In taller enclosures with strong light, some of the dracaenas fare well. Outdoors, we have successfully used large jade plants, elephant bush *(Portulacaria afra)*, tree yuccas, and dracaenas. Interestingly, we have found that in outdoor setups jade plants are particularly favored by these lizards for resting areas.

If you want to add foliage to your bearded dragon vivarium, remember that plants take up space. A large enclosure that is at least 6 feet long is required for combining adult bearded dragons and plants. When placing plants in indoor setups, it is better to introduce them in pots buried in the substrate rather than planting them directly into the substrate. This makes watering possible without wetting the entire setup and helps reduce water loss to the surrounding substrate. It also allows easy removal and replacement of plants as needed.

In terms of design, larger plants are best placed toward the back of the vivarium and smaller ones at midlevel to provide a sense of balance. Generally, placing plants at the base of landscape structures such as rocks or wood will have an attractive, natural effect. Once plants are intro-

Bearded dragon enclosures should be provided with adequate shelter. Photo by David Travis.

duced, the dragons should be monitored closely. Damaging activities such as climbing (it can break branches and topples plants) and attempting to eat plants (which injures or destroys them), tend to occur early on as the dragons explore the new items in their space. Observation should provide you with guidelines for adjustments in plant placement and selection.

Vivarium Maintenance

It is important to monitor your bearded dragon daily to evaluate its attitude, condition, and health and to make sure the vivarium is functioning properly. Bearded dragons are active lizards that eat large amounts of food and consequently defecate correspondingly large amounts. In short, they tend to be messy. For this reason, regular maintenance of a vivarium is a must. With adult dragons, this means regularly using a cat litter scoop to clear fecal material from the substrate. In addition, if water is kept in the enclosure, it should be replaced at least every other day and whenever the container is fouled, especially since dragons may soil the water. The water container should be washed, disinfected (using a 10 percent bleach solution) and thoroughly rinsed on a regular basis to remove accumulating bacterial slime and fecal traces. Assuming the dragons are not kept in crowded conditions, the substrate should be replaced completely about once a month. If paper is used as a substrate, it should be replaced every two to three days, or even daily if necessary. Dirty landscape materials should be removed and disinfected by soaking for a couple of hours in a container with a 10 percent bleach solution, then rinsed and allowed to soak in water to clear traces of bleach.

CHAPTER 4:
THE IMPORTANCE OF HEATING AND LIGHTING

P roviding proper heating and lighting is essential to keeping caged bearded dragons healthy. Their activity and metabolic processes depend on proper light and heat gradients. Without them, your dragons cannot survive.

Heating

Providing adequate heat is critical to the welfare of bearded dragons. The primary source of heat should be a white (not red) incandescent bulb or spotlight in a reflector-type fixture capable of handling the wattage and heat output. A fixture with a ceramic base and no electrical switch in the base typically last longer for this kind of use. Look for a fixture with a switch on the cord, or plug the fixture into a surge suppressor unit and use that switch to turn it on and off. The fixture should be placed on or above the screen top over basking sites such as flat rock or wood. The temperature measured at the site should be 90–100°F, and the bulb wattage should be adjusted to provide the proper tempera-

Many hobbyists choose to include a hot rock type of heater as a secondary heat source when raising baby bearded dragons.

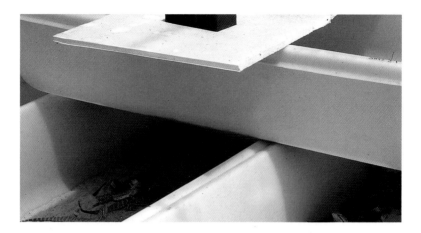

ture. An alternative is to use a higher wattage bulb and wire or plug the fixture into a light dimmer. This allows you to adjust the heat output.

Several bearded dragon specialists recommend combining a hot rock with an overhead spotlight. The temperature at the basking site should measure 90–100°F. Placing rock and other heat absorbing landscape materials under a spotlight can help heat up a basking site more effectively.

As a secondary heat source, a "hot rock" type heater works well with this species and should be placed away from the spotlight heat source unless intentionally combined with a lower wattage incandescent bulb.

During the warmest time of the day when temperatures can reach 100°F, these bearded dragons choose to rest in the shaded portions of their greenhouse enclosure.

Beware of Fire Hazards!

Spotlights generate a great deal of heat and can start a fire if placed too close to combustible materials, such as curtains. We cannot emphasize enough the importance of placing spotlight fixtures securely above the metal screen top of an enclosure and away from curtains and other flammable materials. If you have small children, cats, or other uncaged pets who are likely to topple fixtures or trip on electrical cords, limit access to the room where you keep your bearded dragons. Another cause of fire is placing spotlights on rugs or furniture while doing maintenance. This is especially dangerous when you have a light connected to a timer. Even though the light may be off when you move the fixture, the spotlight will burn whatever lies beneath it when the timer goes on the next day.

Finally, and most important, put a functioning smoke alarm in any room where spotlights or other kinds of heating units are used for reptiles.

Note the central raised keel of the scales, which increases surface area and helps regulate body temperature on this female Sandfire bearded dragon.

Understanding Heat

A key to successfully keeping reptiles is understanding the role of heat. Reptiles are ectotherms, which means that they depend on environmental temperatures to achieve and maintain optimal body temperatures. However, reptiles are not passive in their relationship with environmental temperatures. They thermoregulate by various behaviors including selection among thermal zones.

After a cool night in the desert, a lizard may crawl out into sunlight at midmorning, flatten its body, and adopt an overall darker coloration to increase heat absorption so that it can quickly warm up to an effective operating temperature. This allows it to be alert and fast. Once an optimal temperature is reached, the lizard may hunt insects, perform displays for other lizards, and be wary of potential predators. However, as the midday sun causes air and surface temperatures to rise even higher, the lizard may begin to overheat and will move out of the sun to rest in shade or a shelter until the temperature cools down.

One of the interesting features of reptiles is that that they heat up quickly and cool down relatively slowly. In fact, one of the studies showing this was done with the eastern bearded dragon (Bartholomew and Tucker, 1963). Individuals with a 68° F body temperature placed in a 103° F chamber heated to 101° F in about thirty-eight min-

Killing Them Softly in Small Tanks

FAQ: *I bought a bearded dragon three months ago and I set it up in the 10-gallon tank the pet store sold me along with a spotlight and hot rock. It did well until recently, when it started gaping and stopped feeding. It died two days ago. What happened?*

This is a common scenario when baby bearded dragons are raised in tanks that are too small. Initially, because they are small, they can move away from the heat sources. But as they grow larger, their increased body size makes it impossible to escape the heat. Bearded dragons don't just grow in length, they also grow in height and width, exposing them to more heat than babies. The typical sequence of events is that they first start panting in a desperate attempt to cool off, then they stop eating because survival is becoming their primary concern. Finally, they overheat and die. Because of their rapid growth rate, a 10-gallon tank is not an adequate size for rearing bearded dragons past three to four weeks of age. Next time start with a larger tank.

FAQ: *I recently bought a baby bearded dragon along with a 10-gallon tank and a 100-watt spotlight the pet store recommended. The baby fared well for a couple of weeks and died. What happened?*

This is another common scenario with baby bearded dragons. In a 10-gallon tank, a 100-watt spotlight can generate a temperature over 100°F within most of the dragon's available space. Even if it can initially get away from the heat, before long, as it grows larger, the dragon will be stuck in the hot zone and cook. Bulbs of 60–75 watts will be adequate for smaller tanks, although a 10-gallon tank is not a proper size for rearing baby bearded dragons. Remember what we emphasized earlier: Bearded dragons need a sizeable cool area to escape excessive heat.

We hope this information will emphasize the importance of providing a basking site of around 95°F to allow bearded dragons to thermoregulate. You also will have to provide a cooler, unheated section that they can access once an optimal temperature is achieved. Let bearded dragons choose what to them "feels right." Improper heat gradients are one of the most common causes of illness in bearded dragons and other reptiles.

utes but under reverse conditions required more than fifty minutes to cool from 103° F to 69° F. Thus, a heated reptile can store heat and maintain a relatively high body temperature for an extended period of time.

Optimal temperatures allow efficient metabolism and immune system activity in reptiles. If kept too cool, the metabolic processes of reptiles will occur at a slower rate and the immune system will become depressed. Cool temperatures reduce digestion rate, which can lead to gastrointestinal problems such as decomposition of food in the gut and bloating. The equilibria of bacteria and protozoa in the gut may also be thrown out of balance. Moreover, the rate of clearing uric acid and other compounds through the kidneys is reduced at suboptimal temperatures and the risks of kidney disease increased. Growth rate, which depends on appetite, rapid digestion, and effective metabolism, is directly affected by temperature.

Lighting

Bearded dragons benefit from good lighting. They are less spirited and less active when kept under low light, as you may have seen in pet stores that use ceramic infrared heaters as primary sources of heat. As you probably know, even the moods of humans are affected by low light exposure. How could one expect any less with a sun-loving animal such as the bearded dragon? In addition to spotlights as heat and light sources, full-spectrum or high-UV-B reptile bulbs should be provided from above in fluorescent fixtures that run the length of the enclosure.

The reasoning behind our recommending bulbs that generate UV-B involves vitamins and minerals. It is hypothesized that basking lizards, such as bearded dragons, manufacture vitamin D_3 when exposed to UV-B radiation from sunlight. Because lizards need vitamin D_3 to effectively absorb calcium, lack of this vitamin in the diet or lack of exposure to a UV-B source can lead to calcium deficiency. This becomes very noticeable in baby lizards, which require large amounts of calcium to build rapidly growing skeletons. To prevent this, be sure to provide appropriate amounts of calcium and vitamin D_3 in the diet, along with exposure to UV-B radiation, either via sunlight or special bulbs.

Our observations suggest that bearded dragons eat more, grow faster, and are healthier and more active when provided with sunlight or full-spectrum/reptile UV-B bulbs. In one experiment we had specimens fed ad libitum grow from hatchling to 14 inches long in fourteen weeks by combining a spotlight heat source with full-spectrum

You can make a wooden indoor display with concrete blocks to provide basking sites, nail wearing sites, and a shelter. Provide a spotlight and a UV-B-generating fluorescent bulb. Photo by Val Brinkerhoff, courtesy of Dan McCarron.

Darkness and Feeding

FAQ: *I have a couple of half-grown bearded dragons in a 4-foot tank with a 75-watt spotlight for heat at one end. The problem is that they don't seem interested in eating and they sleep all the time. Should I take them to a veterinarian?*

Don't rush to the clinic just yet. This is another common problem with bearded dragons that are not set up correctly. We see it in pet stores all the time. Bearded dragons are diurnal animals that derive psychological benefits from a high light level. A single spot on a large tank means that most of the tank will be too dark. A consequence of low light is poor appetite.

You should have full-spectrum, high-UV-B, reptile fluorescent bulbs running the length of your tank for up to fourteen hours a day. If after a couple of weeks your dragons don't perk up and show significant improvement in appetite and activity, then you should take them to a qualified reptile veterinarian. Beware, however, of veterinarians inexperienced with bearded dragons. They can sometimes do more harm than good.

bulbs placed 6 inches above the experimental group This growth rate was significantly greater compared to specimens raised under conditions where any of three factors, light-generated heat, UV-B-generating light, and food availability were limited. There are now mercury vapor bulbs sold in the reptile trade that fit incandescent fixtures, produce good levels of UV-B, and emit some heat. They are very effective as a UV source but should not be used as the only heat source because many lizards choose to limit their exposure to high-UV sources. In short, they're great at one end of a large tank with a standard spotlight at the opposite end.

Of course, the inexpensive alternative to UV-generating bulbs is to allow bearded dragons regular exposure to sunlight during the warm months.

Sunlight

The easiest way to provide UV-B is to expose lizards to sunlight. The safest way is to expose them to sunlight to use screen-sided cages, which reduce the risks of overheating. A commonly used alternative is to place bearded dragons in large opaque or white plastic storage containers with a screen top. Glass-sided, clear, or bare-floor plastic containers risk overheating and are often lethal to dragons when placed in the sun. Instead, use sand and cover part with cardboard for shade. Even with screen-sided enclosures, you should always provide an area of shade so your bearded dragon can get out of the sun. Placement of basking cages is also important. Grass or soil is a safe place for these cages. Beware of concrete patios or asphalt surfaces, which build up heat in the sun and can kill your dragons.

Bearded Dragons and UV lighting

FAQ: *Is it possible to raise bearded dragons without using a source of UV light such as the special reptile UV-B bulbs?*

We have raised all three popular species of dragons to adulthood without exposure to UV-B, using regular supplementation with vitamin/mineral mixes that contained calcium and vitamin D_3. However, we feel that raising these lizards without a UV source is a gamble. With the current method of dusting food with powdered vitamin/mineral supplements, we simply don't know enough about the long-term effectiveness of the formulas and proper dosage. By far, the most common health complaint with baby bearded dragons continues to be signs of calcium deficiency such a hind leg twitching. Exposure to a UV source appears to be the most reliable way to provide these lizards with adequate levels of vitamin D_3 to allow absorption of calcium. We also don't know all the other benefits of exposure to a more balanced lighting that comes closer to natural sunlight, including psychological benefits. If you live in a sunny area, exposing your lizards to UV source should be easy and economical during the warmer months of the year. Two to four hours of sunlight a week is probably enough to meet the needs of bearded dragons.

This green-house is set up to house both frilled dragons *(Chlamydosaurus kingii)* and eastern beard-ed dragons *(P. barbata)*. The trees are dra-caenas.

Light, Heat, and Coloration

Proper light and heat can help bring out your dragon's true colors. The bright orange-reds and yellows of certain lines of bearded dragons do not become fully expressed when they are kept indoors. One or more factors related to light conditions (and possibly heat) appear necessary to trigger the hyperxanthic response (an increase in yellow and orange skin pigments). This is comparable to the hyper-melanistic response (increase in dark pigment melanin) of human skin to UV radiation from the sun. The bearded dragons we raise outdoors under greenhouse plastic that filters most of the UV radiation become just as bright as individuals kept in the open, so UV radiation may not nec-essarily be the triggering factor.

Under indoor conditions, we have tried UV-generating reptile bulbs (both fluorescent and mercury vapor) and were unable to get Sandfire dragons to fully color up. However, individuals raised indoors under a combination of mercury-vapor UV-B bulbs (they have a higher UV out-put than fluorescent reptile UV-B bulbs) and incandescent

A Sandfire bearded dragon raised indoors under optimal conditions including spotlights and high UV-B reptile bulbs is remarkably colorful.

spotlights that raised basking site temperatures between 90° and 100° F did develop significantly brighter coloration than animals raised without this combination of heat, UV, and possibly light intensity. That the coloration is a response to external conditions is illustrated by the following example: A group of Sandfire dragons we had sold were bought back after eighteen months because the owner felt their coloration was not up to par. Because we had initially kept back half the clutch of this particular group, we were able to compare the effects of raising conditions. Our greenhouse-raised animals were a bright orange-red while the ones raised indoors were dull with scattered hints of orange. We placed these dull dragons in our greenhouse under plastic and this group steadily brightened, requiring a full three months to achieve the Sandfire coloration.

Winter Shutdown

Once mature (after one year of age), bearded dragons usually enter a state of brumation, commonly termed *shutdown,* in which they remain relatively inactive, hidden in

Winter Shutdown and False Signs of Disease

FAQ: *My bearded dragon had been faring well until last month (November) when it started spending most of its time hidden. It has also refused any food, and I'm worried it may be sick.*

We can't say for sure whether your bearded dragon is actually sick or not. Very likely what you are being faced with is what we call "winter shutdown and the false signs of disease." Indeed, a common reason first-time dragon owners consult veterinarians is winter shutdown. This is a natural rest period for bearded dragons over a year old, and it appears similar to certain signs of disease. Bearded dragons don't feed, they are inactive, and they hide most of the time. When these animals are brought to inexperienced veterinarians, unnecessary, costly, and sometimes harmful procedures are recommended.

To assess the health of your bearded dragon at this time consider the following: If this shutdown occurs in the winter, if your dragon is not losing much weight and is maintaining rounded body contours, if it appears relatively alert and wide-eyed when picked up, then it is probably fine and just doing what bearded dragons naturally do at that time of the year. It's most important for you to keep it at cooler temperatures 66–70° F during this period of time. Only in the case of clear signs of disease such as rapid weight loss, sunken eyes, gaping, forced exhalation, eyes that don't fully open and a limp rag doll feel when held, should a dragon be brought to a veterinarian during apparent winter shutdown.

shelters or lying on the ground and eating little if at all. If raised under indoor conditions, babies hatched out in the summer won't undergo winter shutdown until the following year (at about eighteen months of age). During winter shutdown, dragons must be maintained at cooler temperatures (60–70°F), something easily achieved in most homes by placing the enclosure on the floor of a room during winter months. Basking lights should be reduced to a lower wattage (basking site reduced to 75–80°F) and left on for only eight to ten hours daily. Many owners are alarmed by the drastic change in behavior during this period and believe their dragons may be sick. Winter shutdown, however, is normal for this species. Winter shutdown can last from a few weeks to five months. If bearded dragons are healthy, they will lose little or no weight during this period and will remain in good condition, showing no signs of disease such as sunken eyes, gaping, or twitching.

There are two approaches to winter shutdown. In the

first, the owner can create a shutdown cycle of cooler temperatures and shorter day length, similar to what happens in the wild. Owners need to reduce, then eliminate food for the dragon about one week before the onset of cooler temperatures. Alternatively, an owner can wait and observe the dragon closely, and then create shutdown conditions as soon as the dragon shows signs of reduction in activity and food intake. The end of winter shutdown is marked by a shift in behaviors following the increase in heat and light that accompanies spring. Return dragons to normal conditions as soon as they start basking and feeding again.

Note: Inexperienced veterinarians may fail to recognize winter shutdown and recommend force-feeding during this period. Don't do it. Force feeding at this time is harmful to a dragon.

CHAPTER 5:
DIET AND FEEDING MANAGEMENT

by Susan Donoghue, V.M.D., DACVN, and Philippe de Vosjoli

Bearded dragons consume a wide variety of animal and plant foods throughout their lives. Studies of the stomach contents of wild bearded dragons in Australia showed that when young, these lizards eat about 50 percent live food and 50 percent plants, and when mature, they eat mostly (65–90 percent) plant matter. Observations of thousands of dragons in breeding facilities suggest that similar food preferences occur when these lizards are in captivity. Plan to feed your dragon proportionally more live, moving prey when it is young, and offer relatively more vegetarian fare when it reaches middle and old age.

It is our experience that very young bearded dragons really do need live prey, despite what one may hear or read to the contrary. Without live food, there is a high risk of stunting growth and malnutrition, and even death from starvation. Moreover, baby dragons housed together will cannibalize each other, nipping off toes and tail tips if hungry and deprived of adequate amounts of live prey. If you want a bearded dragon as a pet but won't accept live prey in the house, we suggest that you purchase an older dragon. Young adults and mature dragons can be maintained without live prey, though they greatly enjoy, and we suspect would prefer, occasionally feeding on live food.

The enthusiastic and eclectic appetites of bearded dragons give owners an opportunity to interact with their pets and bring much enjoyment to both species. Food treats can be used as rewards and to attract the attention of a pet

dragon. Many a dragon happily bounds up to an owner when snacks are in hand, and food often serves as the strongest bond between dragon and owner. Dragons are nutritionally robust, handling many food treats and careful diet changes with minimal or easily resolved perturbation of their digestive tracts. Sound diets for dragons have built-in nutritional flexibility that allows for treats and snacks without creating imbalances. We provide guidelines for sound diets and appropriate snacks later in this chapter.

Food and Supplement Sources

Insects

Bearded dragons are usually fed commercially-bred invertebrates such as crickets *(Acheta domestica)*, mealworms *(Tenebrio molitor)*, giant mealworms *(Tenebrio molitor)*, superworms *(Zophobus morio)*, wax worms *(Galleria mellonella)*, and juvenile Madagascar hissing cockroaches *(Gromphodorhina portentos)*. These are available for sale in many pet shops and by mail order.

Bearded dragons cannot be maintained well on flying insects, such as houseflies, which easily evade the dragons. Although dragons may eat earthworms and other garden worms, these prey aren't commonly taken as food.

Vertebrate Prey

Larger bearded dragons do not hesitate to eat small lizards and in fact appear to relish them. In captivity, adults also feed on juvenile (pink to fuzzy) mice. These can be a useful part of a varied diet for larger dragons, providing nutrients such as calcium and many vitamins and trace minerals that are not readily available from invertebrates and salads. Supplementation is unnecessary. Vertebrate prey require balanced diets and water if kept for more than a day.

Greens and Other Produce
Vegetarian foods are available in local markets. Greens, vegetables, and fruits can be offered in appropriate-sized pieces. Generally, finely-chopped produce is accepted best. Plants from fields and lawns that haven't been treated with pesticides and herbicides can be fed, too. Leaves and blossoms from clover, dandelion, and mustard are especially relished. Other treats include many species of grasses and petals from blossoms of roses, hibiscus, and calendula.

Pellets
Commercial diets for bearded dragons are primarily dry pelleted foods. These products may be marketed specifically for bearded dragons or for other pets. Bearded dragons have been raised and maintained successfully when part of their diet has consisted of commercial dry foods formulated and marketed for cats and dogs, and also for other species such as iguanas, tortoises, and cage birds. It is our opinion that no commercial diet, whether marketed for bearded dragons or for other animals, should be the *only* food offered to bearded dragons. Advantages and drawbacks of commercial diets are discussed later in this chapter.

Supplements
Bearded dragons require supplementation with a powdered vitamin/mineral supplement and calcium to make up for deficiencies and high phosphorus levels in commercially produced insects and produce. Reptile supplements are now readily available in stores that sell reptile supplies. Because they vary widely in their formulations, you should carefully examine the labels for contents. Ideally, you should select a source of calcium such as calcium carbon-

ate powder plus a supplement that contains vitamins and minerals including trace minerals. Only small amounts are required—just enough to lightly coat, or dust, insects and plant matter.

Water

Offer high-quality, clean water that is free from contaminants. Generally, water that is safe for you is safe to give your bearded dragon. Most problems with water quality arise from a dragon fouling its water with feces or decomposing food. Be sure to clean the water container daily, and offer clean water at least daily or more often if needed.

Offer water in a shallow dish no more than half the lizard's body height when at rest and wide enough to fit its entire body width. The water must be visible when the dragon is up on all fours. A dragon often enters its water dish and lowers its head to drink.

Bearded dragons (especially babies) are not the brightest lizards when it comes to recognizing water. Generally, they are attracted to the scintillating reflection of light on water droplets or a moving water surface. Because they are attracted to moving water, pouring or dripping water into a container often entices bearded dragons to enter and begin drinking. Spraying the sides of the habitat with water may prove particularly useful for watering babies who, as a rule, don't readily recognize standing water. Dripping water on a bare enclosure floor using a rodent sipper water bottle is another method for tempting dragons to drink. To assure that your bearded dragons get enough water, a good backup method is to manually give them water with a plastic sipper water bottle, slowly squeezing the bottle so that droplets of water fall at the tip of each dragon's snout.

If the above suggestions do not work, an alternative method is to provide no water container in the enclosure but instead remove the dragons and soak them in pans of shallow water two or three times a week.

Water is also obtained through diet. Insects and fresh salads contain about 60 percent and 85 percent water, respectively. Pellets contain only 10–12 percent water, so dragons fed only pellets need to receive enough water each day. Lack of water leads to dehydration and electrolyte disturbances, which seriously impact many organ systems.

High-Quality Food

All foods offered to bearded dragons should be wholesome and either fresh or carefully preserved. Crickets, mealworms, and other invertebrates need to be fed a balanced diet. Breeders have successfully fed them ground dog food, rodent chow, or poultry feed with fresh fruits, greens, and sliced fruit, but now diets specifically formulated to feed crickets are available. Balanced diets, when present in the guts of the insects, make up part of the nutrients absorbed by bearded dragons after prey are consumed. Wax worms need a special diet that includes glycerin, honey, ground cereals, and brewers yeast. Invertebrate enclosures should be cleaned routinely.

Vegetarian foods should be washed prior to feeding if herbicide or pesticide applications are likely. Produce from the market should be checked carefully for hazardous materials such as twist ties, bits of plastic, and rubber bands. These items can lead to life-threatening digestive problems. Remove sticky labels from the surfaces of apples, pears, and the like. Today's frozen vegetables marketed for human consumption are well preserved with little loss of vitamins and other nutrients. These should be thawed before feeding.

Parts of produce intended for human consumption contain lower concentrations of herbicides and pesticides than those parts intended to be discarded and uneaten. Hence, exercise special caution when feeding produce considered inedible by humans, such as rinds from melon and kiwifruit.

The nutritional value of pellets and hay products deteriorates relatively rapidly from exposure to light, air, or heat. For example, levels of beta-carotene, a precursor of vitamin A, fall to less than 50 percent by six months after harvest, yet most commercial pellets and hay products don't reach store shelves until at least several months after hay harvest. We select alfalfa- or clover-based products that still look green.

Supplements have limited shelf lives. Many vitamins decompose from exposure to light, air, and heat. Others are oxidized by contact with trace minerals. We recommend that you select products with expiration dates, and replace supplements at least every four months.

Calcium-Supplemented Dragons That Twitch Their Toes

FAQ: *I set up my baby bearded dragons just right, or so I thought. They are in a room kept at about 80°F with a UV-B emitting bulb. They are fed twice daily with 1/4-inch crickets dusted with calcium and a general vitamin-mineral supplement. This week, a few started twitching, and my vet diagnosed them with calcium deficiency. Where did I go wrong?*

Dietary problems arise as much from errors in husbandry as from diet per se. Years ago, we accidentally induced calcium deficiency in baby dragons kept like yours. The problem wasn't with diet or supplementation but with light and heat. Dragons respond to a *bright* light and a basking spot that is warmer than the overall enclosure. Without stimulation from light, our baby dragons ate a less than optimal number of crickets and developed signs of calcium deficiency. Moreover, such signs don't always have to be due to calcium. Deficiencies of magnesium and glucose can produce similar signs. Whenever you're faced with a nutritional problem, check out husbandry too. For your case specifically, we suggest dropping the room temperature to about 70–75°F and adding a bright light that creates a basking spot of about 90°F. Make sure you retain a temperature gradient so that the dragons can select cooler temperatures, too.

When to Feed

Bearded dragons are active in the daytime and asleep at night. Thus you will want to offer your dragon the bulk of its food in the morning. This is especially important if you are away in the daytime and return home late when the dragon will be sleepy and less interested in eating. The second meal of the day should occur at least an hour or two prior to lights being turned off. Prey that are uneaten and roaming at night can stress or even bite your dragon. Roaming hungry crickets have been known to fatally wound baby dragons.

During winter shutdown, adult bearded dragons are

inactive and may not feed at all. Do not force-feed them at this time. Once your bearded dragons are active again, return to the usual feeding schedule.

How Often to Feed and Water

Bearded dragons are fed frequently when babies, usually two or three times daily. As dragons mature, feeding frequency declines gradually to once daily as young adults. As older adults, they can be fed daily or every other day.

Some successful breeders of bearded dragons offer water only three times weekly. Others maintain water around the clock. Which system is right for you? Bearded dragons evolved in the arid regions of inland Australia and are adapted to dry environments and limited water. Moreover, many of the foods we recommend for dragons, such as invertebrates and salads, contain water. Daily exposure to water is likely unnecessary under certain specific husbandry systems, especially for dragons kept outdoors. However, dragons maintained indoors, especially those in heated homes and those consuming dry pellet foods benefit from daily access to water. We recommend that all pet dragons kept indoors have access to clean water in shallow saucers.

How Much to Feed and Supplement

As a general rule, bearded dragons are fed as many crickets as they can consume in one ten-minute feeding. Adult dragons can be maintained with constant access to invertebrates (during the day) if the prey are confined to a bowl and not free-roaming and creating stress for the dragons. Salads and commercial foods are also available during the day, removing any foods that might decompose at night. Supplements are added carefully to insects and salads, providing just a light coating.

As for size of live prey, bearded dragons almost never suffer from eating prey that are too small. But many dragons, especially babies, have died from eating prey that are too large. A general guideline is to feed crickets that are no longer than the width of the dragon's head. For babies, that

means feeding crickets that are just a week or two old and no more than 1/4-inch long.

As dragons grow, other prey can be fed, but always follow the rule that the prey should be no longer than the width of the dragon's head. Go easy on feeding prey with high chitin content, such as mealworms. However, our dragons relish hard-shelled beetles and we use May beetles and June bugs as treats for adults in early summer. These beetles are too large for juvenile dragons.

The Importance of Dietary Supplements

Most diets for bearded dragons require nutrient supplementation because few of the foods in their diets are nutritionally complete or balanced. Invertebrates (crickets, mealworms, superworms, wax worms) lack calcium because they have no skeleton and are deficient in several vitamins and trace minerals. Vegetarian foods (such as greens, carrots, bananas, etc.) are deficient in a variety of essential nutrients such as calcium and certain amino acids, fatty acids, and trace minerals.

Generally, baby bearded dragons require daily supplementation, and older animals need gradually decreasing rates of supplementation so that they are supplemented weekly or every other week.

The type and amount of supplementation needed by your dragon depends on many factors. For example, dragons housed outdoors with access to the ground obtain the vitamin D_3 from basking in the sun and many trace minerals from access to soil, whereas those kept indoors would need these essential nutrients provided in their diet. We'll cover the most common scenarios for supplementation in this chapter.

Help! My Dragon's Having Convulsions!

FAQ: *I bought a pair of baby bearded dragons a month ago. They've been eating great and growing rapidly. Suddenly, today I found one having convulsions and the other's toes and feet are twitching. What should I do?*

This scenario sounds like a classic case of calcium deficiency in baby dragons. Those babies eating the most and growing the fastest need the most calcium in order to support such rapid growth. Signs of calcium deficiency include tremors, twitching, seizures, and bloating. Give your dragons calcium immediately: we recommend a liquid form, such as Neo-Calglucon (manufactured by Sandoz and available in pharmacies), as the first step for babies that are twitching or having seizures. Consult a reptile veterinarian for dosage and administration. Next, evaluate husbandry and diet. Are your dragons exposed to ample UV-B from sunlight or special bulbs? In our experience, exposure to a reptile mercury vapor UV-B bulb in combination with orally administered calcium is highly efficient, causing improvement in as little as twenty-four hours in bearded dragons and other lizards that display the muscular tremors associated with calcium deficiency. Do they have a source of dietary calcium and dietary vitamin D_3? You may need the help of a qualified veterinarian to correct the immediate problem of hypocalcemia and for advice on fixing the dragons' husbandry and diet.

Supplemental Calcium

Calcium is critical for healthy bone growth in bearded dragons. You'll want to feed your dragons foods high in calcium, but dragons need supplemental calcium as well, regardless of diet. (However, if you feed your dragons *only* balanced and complete dry pelleted diets then you don't need to supplement.) Most supplements emphasizing vitamins and minerals fail to provide enough calcium to meet the needs of dragons. Thus, two types of supplements are often necessary: one containing vitamins and minerals (including a little calcium) and the other containing mainly calcium (such as calcium carbonate, bonemeal, and cuttlebone).

Dragons needing the most calcium are babies and egg-laying females. Appropriate rates of supplementation vary with the dragon's age and size, housing (indoors or out), calorie intake, amount of calcium provided by the diet, and amounts of several other nutrients in the diet, including phosphorus and vitamin D_3. Generally, baby dragons are supplemented with calcium daily or every second day, and rates decrease with increasing age and size.

Bearded dragons require 1–1.5 percent of the diet dry matter as calcium, and about 0.5–0.9 percent phosphorus. Attention is often given to the ratio of calcium to phosphorus in the diet. It should be in the range of 1:1 to 2:1 calcium:phosphorus (Ca:P). However, the *amounts* of dietary calcium and phosphorus are more important than the ratio. For example, if a diet contained only 0.4 percent calcium and 0.2 percent phosphorus, the Ca:P ratio would be 2:1 but the amounts are deficient and a dragon fed this diet would develop calcium deficiency.

Of the commonly available calcium supplements, calcium content is 40 percent in calcium carbonate, 38 percent in limestone, 18 percent in calcium lactate, and 9 percent in calcium gluconate. Calcium and phosphorus contents are 24 percent and 12 percent in bonemeal, and 24 percent and 18 percent in dicalcium phosphate.

Supplemental Vitamin D

Bearded dragons require vitamin D for a variety of functions, including the formation of strong bones by aiding the absorption of dietary calcium. Dietary vitamin D comes in two forms—vitamin D_2 (ergocaciferol), which occurs in plants, and vitamin D_3 (cholecalciferol), which occurs in animal tissue, especially liver. There is evidence that reptiles cannot utilize vitamin D_2, so vitamin D_3 is always recommended for bearded dragons. Basking lizards such as bearded dragons can also make vitamin D_3 by exposing their skin to UV-B light rays from the sun or from special commercial lamps. We know of no scientific data demonstrating the relative value to dragons of vitamin D_3 obtained from diet or from UV-B exposure.

Although some dragons seem to do well without dietary vitamin D if they live outdoors year-round, we recommend a source of dietary D_3 for most bearded dragons, especially those living all or part of the year indoors. Vitamin D_3 is listed on food labels as cholecalciferol, animal sterol, D-activated animal sterol, irradiated animal sterol, or vitamin D_3. Don't assume that the term "vitamin D" in the label ingredient list is actually D_3, for it may be D_2 and unusable by your dragon.

As with many nutrients, vitamin D is toxic when fed in excess. Toxicity most commonly occurs from overzealous supplementation with vitamin-mineral products. Toxicity also occurs from the ingestion of certain types of rat and mouse poisons. Signs of toxicity often involve multiple organ systems because of widespread soft-tissue calcification. The active form of vitamin D is made by a series of chemical transformations in liver and then kidney. Thus diseases of the liver or kidney will affect vitamin D metabolism and can lead to signs of deficiency or toxicity.

Disorders caused by too little or too much vitamin D, or diseases of the liver and kidney, which lead to secondary problems with vitamin D, require veterinary attention.

Feeding Guidelines: An Age-by-Age Guide

Baby Bearded Dragons

Newly hatched bearded dragons may take a day or two to begin eating. During this time, the baby receives needed nutrition from its own reserves, mostly through its resorbed yolk sac. The youngster should be housed in a small enough enclosure so that it can find its food and water.

Babies should be started on one- to two-week-old crickets and graduated to larger crickets as they grow older. Offer the baby dragon only a few live, small (about 1/8-inch) crickets. To determine appropriate cricket size, figure the crickets should have a length no greater than the width of the head of a bearded dragon. Offering a larger number of smaller prey promotes more efficient digestion than offering a smaller number of larger prey.

Greens and vegetables should be offered daily, finely chopped *(left)* for baby bearded dragons and coarsely chopped *(right)* for adults.

Observe the baby dragon to ensure that it is eating. Within a day or two of hatching, a baby dragon should be a lively feeder. Don't overload the tank with crickets, which will stress the dragon. Loose crickets will crawl over the lizard and may bite it.

Crickets should be offered two to three times daily. Observe that the bearded dragon is eating and offer only enough crickets that can be eaten in one feeding (within about ten minutes).

Drinking water should be provided in shallow saucers; we use inverted plastic can covers. Very young hatchlings are often thirsty but can have trouble finding water in a large enclosure. Lightly misting the walls and enclosure furnishings or dripping water into a saucer can help baby dragons to begin drinking. The goal is to provide drinking water for the hatchlings, not to create a humid environment or standing puddles of water.

Crickets should be dusted once a day with a mixture of powdered calcium carbonate and a vitamin-mineral supplement. This is most easily accomplished by placing an allotment of crickets into a smooth-sided container from which they can't escape, such as a glass jar or plastic pitcher, then adding an amount of supplement appropriate to

the number of crickets to be fed out. As a rule of thumb, a small pinch of supplement will be adequate to coat the insects for feeding two to three baby dragons; for larger dragons figure a large pinch per animal or an eighth of a teaspoon for a trio. Then gently stir the container for a few seconds until the crickets are lightly coated with the supplement, and feed the crickets to your hungry dragon.

It helps to introduce new foods when such young lizards are inquisitive. Offer finely chopped greens and commercial foods crumbled into bite-sized pieces daily (inverted plastic tops from containers work well as food trays), and leave them in the enclosure throughout the day. The baby dragons will run through the food and often ignore it initially. As the days pass, however, the dragons will nibble on these foods and begin to include them as part of the daily intake.

Uneaten food, including spared crickets, should be removed at the end of each day. Water should be changed daily, and dirty water should be replaced more often as needed.

We recommend that no snacks or treats be offered to very young dragons. These lizards are growing rapidly and need to fill up on highly nutritious supplemented crickets if they are to achieve their genetic potential for size, conformation, and performance. The dragons themselves are less

One of the proposed benefits of making veggies plentiful is to reduce intraspecies mutilations by curbing hunger. Photo by Roger Klingenberg.

interested in snacks during this phase. The focus of the baby dragons should also be the focus of the owner—providing enough well-supplemented crickets in a hospitable, wholesome environment to allow for optimal development.

Common feeding problems at this stage include starvation and malnutrition. Starvation is characterized by poor growth, loss of weight, and often death. It is due to poor food intake arising from a variety of causes that can include: temperatures too cool and/or lighting too dim, which will inhibit the feeding response; feeding inappropriate foods, such as offering only salad, only commercial pellets, or crickets too large for the young dragon to eat; and large, rapidly growing dragons that may be bullying slower-growing dragons, reducing food intake in the runts.

A secondary problem from inadequate food intake is mutilation. Hungry baby dragons will nip the toes and tail-tips of other dragons. If this is observed, add an additional daily meal or increase the amount of crickets fed at each meal.

Malnutrition occurs from feeding imbalanced diets, such as unsupplemented crickets. Calcium deficiency is common, arising from deficiencies of dietary calcium and/or dietary vitamin D_3 or UV-B. Young dragons with symptoms of calcium deficiency (shaking, twitching, paralysis, or lameness) need veterinary treatment and diet evaluation.

Juveniles (Two to Four Months)

During this stage, young bearded dragons are eating machines. Growth is very rapid—bearded dragons increase their size more than 4000 percent in their first six months under optimal conditions. Crickets of an appropriate size (two to four weeks old, 1/4 to 1/2 inch) should be offered twice daily in amounts that are consumed in about ten minutes. Crickets should be supplemented every second or third meal, depending in part on the product that is used and the growth rate of the dragon.

Introduce other small invertebrates. Dragons enjoy wax worms and mealworms. Newly molted mealworms contain less chitin, and are more digestible. These, too, should be supplemented since they also lack calcium and other essential nutrients.

Offer salads of finely chopped greens and vegetables. The overall best green in our opinion is romaine because it is palatable, nutritious, and contains moderate calcium (0.7 percent), beta-carotene (over 50 retinol equivalents per gram dry matter), and fiber (35 percent). Romaine lettuce (with appropriate supplements) has been fed successfully to bearded dragons through all life stages. Other greens can be mixed in too, including dandelion, mustard, collard, kale, leaf lettuces, and bagged mixes of salad greens. These too should be supplemented to provide missing essential nutrients, especially calcium but also trace minerals, vitamins, and fiber.

Dragons enjoy colorful chopped fruits and vegetables mixed into their greens. Figs, kiwifruit sections, apples, berries, green peas, banana, and green beans can be fed in small amounts.

High-Calcium Foods	Poor Calcium Sources
alfalfa and clover hays (1.5 percent)	alfalfa sprouts (0.3 percent)
dandelion greens (1.3 percent)	figs (0.2 percent)
mustard greens (1.3 percent)	peas (0.1 percent)
spinach (1.1 percent)	melons (0.1 percent)
kale (0.8 percent)	mango (0.06 percent)
romaine (0.7 percent)	apple (0.05 percent)
	papaya (0.02 percent)
	banana (0.02 percent).

As a general rule, high-calcium foods cannot be fed in great enough quantities to make up for the deficiencies of the other, calcium-deficient foods in a dragon's diet. Supplementation with calcium is almost always needed.

Commercial diets may be offered, too. These should be crumbled or moistened if pellet size is too large. Moistened foods need to be changed daily in order to avoid mold and decomposition.

FAQ: My friend told me that spinach and kale are bad for dragons, but mine loves these foods. Can I still feed these greens?

All greens contain substances generally referred to as secondary plant compounds. Some are helpful to animals, and others can be harmful. Two substances most frequently mentioned are oxalates and goitrogens, but there are many other compounds, some more risky than these two. If you avoided every green, fruit, and vegetable that contains a potentially harmful secondary plant compound, there would be nothing left to feed! You can continue to feed spinach and kale to your dragon. Make sure they make up just a moderate part of the overall diet and that you include supplements containing calcium and trace minerals. Don't feed diets of just spinach and kale with no additional supplementation.

During the juvenile stage, a variety of foods can be offered occasionally (no more than one or two bite-sized pieces every one or two days) as snacks and treats. These can be bits of watermelon, cucumber, papaya, cantaloupe and other melons, and mango. We know of pet bearded dragons that enjoy *small amounts* of turkey and cranberries on Thanksgiving and a tiny piece of fruit pie on other holidays. Care must be taken to keep the portions small. No supplementation is needed for occasional snacks.

Common nutritional problems seen at this stage include underfeeding because the offered prey are too large for the dragon. Consumption of too-large crickets may be also associated with partial paralysis. Owners sometimes want to rush into larger crickets, but be patient. Pushing baby bearded dragons to their limit on prey size is risking serious problems.

Calcium deficiency is often seen at this stage. Parasitic and infectious diseases may result from failure to keep food and water scrupulously clean. Juvenile dragons are quite active and they'll frequently scamper through food and water, soiling everything in their path. A part of feeding management is maintenance of hygienic conditions.

Subadult (Four Months to Sexual Maturity)

In this stage of adolescence, offer crickets once or twice a day. As the dragon grows, the size of cricket can increase gradually up to adult size, which is 1 inch at six weeks. Crickets should be supplemented every second or third day, depending in part on the product that is used and the growth rate of the dragon.

Superworms are enjoyed, as are juvenile cockroaches (ones farmed as food animals; not captured pests that may be carrying pesticide residues) and young mice (both pink and fuzzy). These prey animals are enjoyed by most dragons and are conducive to but not essential for good health.

Salads become a more substantial part of diet at this stage, so more attention needs to be given to their nutritional balance. Appropriate greens include romaine and other lettuces, kale, mustard, collard, and the like. Vegetables include varieties of beans and other legumes (such as peas), corn, sweet potato, yam, and squash. Fruits include banana, melon, apple, papaya, and berries. All components of the salad need to be chopped into bite-sized pieces suited to the size of your dragon. The salad should be supplemented with a light sprinkling of at least calcium. The nutritional quality of the salad improves if it is supplemented with appropriate amounts of amino acids, fatty acids, insoluble fibers, vitamins, and minerals.

Chopped hays and alfalfa pellets may be added to salads, supplying a source of insoluble fiber as well as calcium and protein. Select products that are still green and haven't faded. Owners occasionally use alfalfa hay or pellets as enclosure substrates for their dragons. Although use of these foods reduces risks of intestinal blockage from ingestion of substrate, these products mold readily in the presence of moisture (from spilled water, fresh salads, excretory products, and misted water), which risks digestive upsets and pneumonia if the mold spores are consumed or inhaled.

Nutritional upsets may arise from overfeeding snacks and treats. Excessive intake of just one food (such as apples, berries, or meat), can lead to diarrhea. Usually, digestive upsets are self-contained and resolve within a day. Occasionally, serious gastrointestinal disease and dehydration develop, necessitating veterinary treatment. Owners

may be alarmed by a change in the color of their dragon's stool, but this often reflects simply the passage of pigments (such as orange carotenoids) from vegetables or dyes from commercial pellets.

Adults

Adult bearded dragons should be offered four- to six-week-old crickets and/or superworms daily or every second day. Other prey for occasional feeding can include mealworms, wax worms, and other commercially farmed invertebrates, such as grasshoppers, locusts, and other field-collected insects (make sure the fields and lawns haven't been treated) and small vertebrates such as young mice. Adult dragons also relish young lizards, so should never be allowed access to pet baby dragons in the household.

Supplemented salads should be offered daily or every second day. Commercial diets are often offered free choice (kept available so that the lizards always have access). Generally, bearded dragons are allowed to eat as much of their salads and commercial diets as they wish. This works well as long as each is nutritionally balanced and complete. Alternatively, vertebrate prey or well-supplemented invertebrate prey may be used to make up latent dietary deficiencies of the commercial products.

Snacks and treats may be offered in very small portions

that can be swallowed in one gulp once or twice daily. These can include the fruits and vegetables your dragon especially likes or even food from the table (see our limitations elsewhere in this chapter).

Nutritional disorders may occur in adult dragons, especially those newly acquired by inexperienced owners. These disorders are usually due to failure to supplement or failure to provide adequate temperature and lighting, thus reducing food intake. Occasionally, oversupplementation occurs when adults are fed large numbers of crickets supplemented daily with products meant to be used only once or twice weekly. Supplements most likely to cause nutrient toxicities are those containing proportionately greater amounts of vitamin A, vitamin D_3, and certain trace minerals such as zinc, copper, and iron. Calcium can also be provided in excess, leading to constipation and, if prolonged, secondary deficiencies of zinc, copper, and iodine. Excessive ingestion of calcium-containing sand used for substrate has caused intestinal impaction and death in bearded dragons.

Females may consume less food in late pregnancy because the eggs fill much of the coelomic space. During this time, the female should be offered the foods she especially enjoys eating, with attention given to digestibility and the nutritional balance of those foods. Crickets and other prey provide more calories and high-quality protein than salads or many commercial diets, so supplemented invertebrates may be especially valuable foods at this time. Despite the best of care, females often mobilize their own body stores in late pregnancy. After egg-laying, these body stores need to be replenished, and a nutritious diet should be offered daily. We prefer live invertebrates as part of this diet, along with salads.

Senior Bearded Dragons
Until data from feeding trials on aged bearded dragons are available, we offer recommendations based on the science of geriatric nutrition and our own experiences with old dragons. Senior bearded dragons tend to be less active, so

they need fewer calories. However, their needs for essential nutrients remain at or near levels of younger, nonbreeding dragons. So our goals are to offer fewer calories but to maintain high-quality diets. This is accomplished most easily by offering free choice, nutritionally balanced salads daily, and feeding limited amounts of crickets and super-worms. The prey are offered every second or third day, and feeding rates and amounts are adjusted according to the dragon's body condition.

Feeding Only Commercial Diets

A number of commercial diets are marketed specifically for bearded dragons. These are comprised of plant- and animal-based ingredients usually in the form of extruded (and occasionally compressed) pellets. Most contain dyes to enhance colors, and many have sprayed-on odors (marketed erroneously as "flavors") to enhance acceptance by owners as much as dragons.

These products are relatively new, and information about testing in feeding trials is limited or lacking. Because the adequacy of these diets is uncertain, we do not recommend any as the sole source of food for bearded dragons at this time.

Several characteristics are common to all pellets, regardless of the formulation or quality control in manufacture. All pellets contain minimal water—about 10–12 percent. In contrast, the water content of fresh salads is about 85–92 percent and the water content of invertebrates is about 60–70 percent. A dragon fed only pellets is receiving much less water from its food than it should. It is possible (but not yet established) that dragons can compensate by drinking proportionally more water. This means even more attention must be given to providing clean, high-quality water to dragons at all times. On the other hand, it is also possible that dragons *cannot* compensate for a reduced water intake, which predisposes them to kidney disease from chronic dehydration.

Most pellets utilize the ingredients and production techniques of the commercial livestock and pet food industries. The formulations meet the needs of manufacturing first and dragons second, using ingredients readily available in the feed industry. While these features aren't inherently bad for dragons, they limit the scope and breadth of feeding such enthusiastic, interactive lizards. The ingredients in pellets are relatively few (corn, soy, poultry meal, tallow, alfalfa, wheat, and the like), whereas the palates of bearded dragons range through a myriad of foods. The deficiencies in pellet ingredient variety is compensated for by differing shapes and dyes, which may please the eye of the owner more than the palate of bearded dragons.

All pellets contain relatively little fat; about 10 or 12 percent is the limit for commercial pellets sold in paper and cardboard containers. Salads contain even less fat. In contrast, invertebrates contain 30–60 percent fat. This fat is essential for bearded dragon nutrition, providing needed calories for growth, reproduction, and good health, along with essential fatty acids for development of vital tissues, especially brain. We know of breeders observing poor growth in juvenile dragons who had been fed low-fat and relatively low-protein pellets. The dragons improved markedly once the diet was changed to a pellet with more fat.

Another type of commercial dry food has been fed successfully to bearded dragons—dry dog and cat foods. Many of these foods contain enough fiber and levels of fat and high-quality protein, which support growth and reproduction. However, we do not recommend feeding cat food to bearded dragons. Modern commercial cat foods are formulated to produce the excretion of acid (to maintain cat urinary health), which increases calcium excretion, predisposing a bearded dragon to calcium deficiency. Dog foods are not formulated in this way, and should help to maintain calcium balance and good bone in dragons. If owners insist on feeding a pellet, we suggest that dry dog food should serve as only one-half of a dragon's feeding regimen, although we prefer a diet of supplemented invertebrates and fresh salads.

In mammalian species, feeding only pellets has led to digestive disorders (in herbivores and omnivores) from a lack of long-stem fibers, poor growth (in omnivores and carnivores) from a lack of fat, and behavioral disorders (in all species) from the monotony of the diet. So owners wishing to feed only pellets to bearded dragons should be cautious and observant.

If you wish to feed your dragon a strictly commercial diet with no crickets or salads, do not try this before the dragon is two to four months of age and even later is better. The changeover must be gradual, with free-choice offering of the commercial product (offered fresh daily), and gradual removal of other foods over several weeks.

Health Problems Related to Diet

Assessing the Diet

Owners can assess the adequacy of their dragon's diet by careful observation. A well-fed bearded dragon appears plump and relatively well muscled. There is a slight paunch to the dragon's belly. Pelvic bones should be barely visible in older juveniles and young adults, but the very young, very old, and actively breeding females may exhibit pelvic bones with only a modest covering of subcutaneous fat. Tails should be wide at the base and well fleshed.

A well-fed dragon is alert and aware of activity in its surroundings. It should actively move about the enclosure, choosing at various times to bask, eat, dig into substrate, and soak in its water dish. The dragon should eagerly eat live food and enjoy salads too. Stools should be formed rather than sloppy. Like other meat-eaters, dragon feces may have a pungent odor, even when the individual is healthy.

An exception to the above description is when the bearded dragon is shutting down for winter but is otherwise healthy. Food intake and activity is greatly reduced in lizards at this time. Weight loss, however, should be minimal.

What not to Feed

Never feed lightning bugs (fireflies) to your bearded dragon. These are highly toxic, resulting in rapid death of a bearded dragon after the consumption of even one firefly. Also, avoid feeding spiders known to be venomous to man, such as black widow and brown recluse spiders.

The toxicity of avocado to bearded dragons is unknown, but it is toxic to cage birds. Do not feed any part of an avocado plant to a bearded dragon until its toxicity in reptiles has been determined. Avoid feeding wild unidentified mushrooms and wild, brightly colored, unidentified berries. It's best to avoid feeding plants known to be toxic to mammals, such as bracken fern, equisetum, buttercup, poppy, rhododendron and the like. Most houseplants should be avoided, but pothos is safe (if untreated) and greatly enjoyed by bearded dragons.

Also avoid foods containing theobromine (in tea and chocolate), alcohol (in certain candies, drinks, vanilla and other flavorings), and caffeine (in tea, coffee, soft drinks). Some foods are not toxic but may lead to digestive or metabolic upset in bearded dragons because of high sugar content or the presence of artificial sweeteners. Avoid feeding candies, soft drinks, and sports drinks to your dragon.

While processed foods for people, such as pizza, nachos,

Mystery Deaths

FAQ: *I thought I was doing what's best for my dragons, but now two are dead! They've been outside for the summer in a screen cage set up with ample shade and areas to bask in the sun. I feed and water them before work each morning and hose out the cage each evening. Last night, about an hour after cage cleaning, I found two of them dead! I know they were feeling okay because they still had bugs in their mouths. What happened?*

While we can't make diagnoses long distance, we're suspicious that your dragons died from eating fireflies. These insects, also known as lightning bugs, are especially prevalent in the eastern U.S., are active in the evening, and seem to be attracted to damp grass and foliage. We know one breeder who lost dozens of adult dragons one summer during a drought, when he began hosing the cages in the evening. Fireflies would then enter the cages and be gobbled up by the dragons. It only takes one firefly to kill a dragon, and death occurs very soon after swallowing the bug. We suggest that you change your routine, hosing the cages in the morning, prior to feeding, and offering another meal in late afternoon (with no additional hosing) to offset late-day dragon hunger.

and cheeseburgers, are not generally recommended for bearded dragons, the *occasional* small nibble will likely do little or no physical harm and may provide a little cement to the human-pet bond.

Secondary Plant Compounds

Plants play a major role in the nutrition of bearded dragons. Plants, however, contain much more than just nutrients. A broad category of substances, termed secondary plant compounds, impacts the feeding of dragons.

Oxalates bind calcium and trace minerals in the digestive tract, preventing their absorption and risking deficiency. Oxalates are found in varying amounts in spinach, rhubarb, cabbage, peas, potatoes, beet greens, and many other plants. These foods do *not* have to be avoided entirely, for nutritional deficiencies are risked only when these foods are fed frequently or as the sole source of nutrition without supplementation. Provision of the usual supplements of calcium and trace minerals and offering a varied diet eliminates most risk.

Goitrogens bind the trace mineral iodine, risking goiter or hypothyroidism. Goitrogens are found in highest quantities in cabbage, kale, mustard, turnip, rutabaga, and other cruciferous plants. These foods can be fed as part of a varied diet along with provision of a supplement that contains iodine (which can be as simple as iodized table salt or, better, iodized "lite" salt containing iodine, sodium, potassium, and chloride). Many commercial supplements contain adequate levels of iodine. The mineral iodine is itself toxic in large quantities (also acting as a goitrogen), so care should be taken not to overdose with commercial supplements, iodized salt, or kelp.

There are many other secondary plant compounds, and it is unfortunate that oxalates and goitrogens receive more attention than needed, while other substances are ignored. For example, many plants contain substances with hormonelike activity (such as phytoestrogens in soybeans) which may impact bearded dragon reproduction. A large number of different plant fibers may affect bearded dragon digestion and intestinal health. Other compounds in plants influence cognitive function, acting as stimulants or sedatives. A general rule for feeding plants to bearded dragons is to offer a variety of produce from local markets of the kind and quality that you yourself would eat. Supplement this produce with calcium and other essential nutrients. And include prey as part of a varied, balanced diet.

Other Factors Affecting Nutrition

The suggestions we've made here are general guidelines, and many factors will affect the diet and feeding management of dragons in specific situations. For example, those housed outside year-round with exposure to natural sunlight certainly don't need UV-B-generating bulbs and may not need a dietary source of vitamin D_3. They may consume trace minerals from the soil, and an array of secondary plant compounds if offered wild plants. These dragons will have nutritional needs that differ from a pet dragon housed indoors full-time.

Feeding regimens may have to be adjusted, depending on your dragon's condition, its environment, and your management. A change of enclosure or adding cage mates, for example, can alter feeding responses, as can the dragon's attainment of sexual maturity.

Females that are bred every year will have greater nutritional demands than a solitary pet that never reproduces. Breeding females are subjected to an obvious stress, and stress itself increases nutrient demands, even in the absence of reproduction. Stress may be insidious and not immediately obvious to dragon owners. For example, stress can arise from chronic excessive exposure to vibrations or light, too much handling or rough handling, or unwanted attention by the family dog or cat.

Illness affects nutrition, too. Bearded dragons that are sick or in pain often don't want to eat, which can impair recovery from illness and surgery. Disease itself impacts nutritional needs, and dragons may lose weight when sick, even though food intake has been maintained.

Bearded dragons can be underfed or overfed. Generally,

young animals are most at risk for underfeeding because they are growing so rapidly. Many cases of underfeeding are due to errors in husbandry. Adult dragons are most at risk for overfeeding because their growth and activity have slowed. Carefully observe your dragon's body condition accordingly, adjusting the amounts of foods offered to avoid under- and overfeeding.

Bearded dragons are susceptible to nutrient deficiencies and excesses. The most common is metabolic bone disease, caused by a deficiency of calcium and/or vitamin D_3. It can be prevented by supplementing crickets and salads with calcium (calcium carbonate is inexpensive and widely available) and vitamin D_3, and by exposing dragons to natural sunlight and UV-B-generating bulbs.

Oversupplementation of certain vitamins and minerals can pose risks of toxicity. This is more likely in adults, so care should be taken to reduce supplementation schedules as your dragon grows older. Excessive supplementation with calcium, without provision of adequate levels of trace minerals, risks secondary deficiencies of zinc, copper, and iodine.

Excessive feeding of snacks and treats risks dietary imbalance and nutritional deficiencies as well as digestive upsets. Limit snacks to small portions, and offer no more than once or twice daily. The goal is to limit snacks and treats to about 10 percent of the total daily food intake.

There is not one right way to feed all bearded dragons. However, careful application of the guidelines in this books and observation of your dragon, with consideration of your husbandry style, will result in a well-fed dragon.

CHAPTER 6:

THE BEARDED DRAGON AS A PET

by Susan Donoghue, D.V.M., D.A.V.C.N., and Philippe de Vosjoli

We are often asked, "Honestly, how good a pet is a bearded dragon?" The answer: They might just be the overall best reptile pet! Unlike many other lizards, dragons almost never bite their handlers, scratch when held, or whip with their tails when approached. They offer a unique and charming personality and natural curiosity about the world around them, including their owners. As your dragon matures, you'll find it making eye contact with you, approaching for food tidbits, and remaining quiet and friendly when held for short periods.

Dragons are ideal because they provide the pleasure and entertainment of a pet that enjoys, but doesn't always require, interaction with humans. They won't develop neuroses if they're not handled or given attention daily, unlike other pets such as dogs and parrots. Bearded dragons are sizeable but not too large. They're aesthetically complex and different enough to draw attention. They display a wide range of social behaviors when kept in groups. They're also characters that sometimes demonstrate endearing signs of intelligence and responsiveness.

In terms of care, drawbacks may include their need for large enclosures, expensive lighting, and insects for food. They also require maintenance of about ten or fifteen minutes a day, minimum. Whether the drawbacks are worth the enjoyment is something that must be assessed by prospective owners.

Handling

Hatchlings and baby bearded dragons are fragile and easily crushed, so they should not be handled (except for health checks) until they are at least 8 inches long. Care should be taken with all juveniles, for they can be seriously hurt from falling onto hard surfaces. Dragons also risk overheating when exposed to sunlight and chilling when exposed to cold. During the first eight weeks of a dragon's life, the most responsiveness you should expect is food taken from your hands. If they incidentally climb on you, great, but keep your hand above or within the enclosure.

After a bearded dragon reaches a length of eight inches, you will be able to handle it more frequently but only for brief periods each time. In terms of handling, bearded dragons don't enjoy long-term holding and petting. Their skin is rough to the touch and not that inviting to pet anyway. If physical contact with a pet is important to you, relatively few lizards fit the bill, with perhaps smooth-skinned blue-tongue skinks being among the best candidates.

You should never allow your bearded dragons to be loose outdoors even if perched on a shoulder. They can fall, or become frightened and dart off. If they escape, dragons are easy prey for dogs, cats, large birds, and cars. If you must carry an adult bearded dragon around with you, then invest in a lizard harness. Remember that many people are afraid of reptiles and you should take this into consideration whenever displaying your reptiles in public. We are opposed to displaying reptiles in public outside of a proper forum such as shows and educational displays.

Hand-Feeding

Bearded dragons are not drawn to humans because of social propensity (like dogs who look to their owner as the alpha member of their social group) or because they enjoy physical contact or good conversation. They do however quickly learn to associate humans with one of their favorite activities—eating. Regularly offering food held by fingertips or within your hand (hand-feeding) is important for establishing a positive relationship between owner and dragon. Hand-feeding can be done early on when bearded dragons are just a few weeks old. In time, they will learn to come toward you as you approach the enclosure, for they begin to associate you with tasty goodies.

A question we're often asked concerns training of dragons to perform tricks. Based on work using food as a positive reinforcement with other lizards, it appears that bearded dragons could also be trained to a much greater degree than commonly believed. We look forward to reports of learning and training in this species.

Dragon Hygiene and Grooming

No matter how large you make your dragon's living quarters, an enclosure still isn't the wide open space of the great outdoors. A pet dragon remains in relatively close contact to its excreted feces and urates, leftover food, fouled water, and old substrate. Such close contact makes for a soiled dragon at best, and risks disease at times. This is why cleanliness is so important. We've mentioned the need for regular cage cleaning. How about dragon cleaning?

Dragons that are soiled from feces or bedding can be

Bearded dragons shed their skin in sheets, much like humans do after a sunburn. Photo by David Travis

bathed. Place your dragon in a plastic container (such as a plastic storage tub) containing an inch or two of slightly warm water. Soap is unnecessary. Using a soft toothbrush, nailbrush, or wash cloth, gently scrub the dirty areas. Rinse in clean, warm water. Once a brush or cloth is designated for dragon use, never use it again on humans.

Dragons shed their skin in small patches. This occurs routinely throughout the year and is normal. You don't need to assist the dragon by peeling off loose skin. Refrain from the temptation to use hand lotions and oils on dragon skin. The loose skin will shed in its own time, at the right time. Occasionally, however, shed skin may become stuck around tails and toes. Then your dragon needs assistance because the remaining bands of dead skin can constrict blood flow and lead to death of cells in the extremities. Soaking and gently peeling often removes the ring of skin. If the skin doesn't come off, have your dragon seen by a qualified veterinarian. If the problem recurs frequently, review your husbandry, especially humidity levels and access to water.

Dragon nails stay short and strong if exposed to rocks and coarse pebbles. Dragons that live on soft surfaces may need their long nails clipped occasionally. The staff at your

Bearded Dragons and Skin Shedding

FAQ: *I've had an adult bearded dragon for more than a year and have yet to see it shed its skin. Do bearded dragons shed?*

Like other reptiles, bearded dragons regularly shed their epithelial skin in a single sheet, much like we do after a sunburn. Most reptiles tend to shed frequently when young and less often as they get older. Injury or disease to the skin also results in increased shedding rate to repair the damage. One way to recognize when a bearded dragon is about to shed is that its coloration appears duller, as if covered with a clear white film. This is a sign of the old skin layer being pushed to the surface and separated from the underlying replacement skin. Bearded dragons shed in broken skin patches that they apparently eat. The various breeders we've talked to have said that they have seldom seen bearded dragons actually shedding or found shed skins in their enclosures. Very likely the skin is quickly consumed after shedding. A clue that this may be what actually happens can be observed in baby bearded dragons. When keeping babies in a group, it is not uncommon to see one pick the shedding skin off of another. Possibly the same happens with adults.

FAQ: *I have a sick baby bearded dragon that is having trouble shedding. Is this common in bearded dragons?*

In bearded dragons, various factors can sometimes cause problems in shedding, including disease, diet, and husbandry conditions. Sick reptiles may be too weak to perform the movements required to remove shed skin, so it is not unusual to see sick dragons with adhering shed skin. Injuries to the skin that result in scabs or scars can also cause localized adhesion of old skin. Substrates may play a role in helping free shed skin from digits, which is why more natural substrates are often recommended. Diet including water and vitamin/mineral content of food can also play a role in rates of shedding and facilitating shedding. Providing a varied diet that includes fresh greens and vegetables will help prevent shedding problems.

To remove adhering skin from a sick dragon, keep it on paper substrate and gently mist it with lukewarm water to help soften the adhering skin. Then try gently peeling loose skin using fingertips or tweezers. It is important that you only attempt to remove loose, white shed skin that is clearly in the process of coming off. Removing skin during the milky stage when new skin is still forming can cause serious skin injuries.

veterinarian's office can perform this task for you, or you can clip the nails yourself. Use a small nail clipper made for cats, and always have coagulant powder handy. Remove just the tip, taking care to avoid the quick. If the nail bleeds, apply coagulant powder or styptic pencil, and try taking less off each remaining nail.

We know of kids who have painted their dragons' nails. These "punk lizards" seem no worse for the experience as long as the nail polish is approved for use in people. Body paints and body piercing, however, are off limits.

Traveling with Your Bearded Dragon

Over the years that you'll own a dragon, it's likely that your pet may have to travel. There may be need for a visit to the veterinarian's office, and your lizard may accompany you to school for a project, move to a new home with the family, or come along on vacation.

Bearded dragons travel well inside small plastic cat carriers. These are available wherever pet supplies are sold. It's best to purchase the carrier ahead of time so that you can acclimate your dragon to the new smells and confined space. Place an old bath towel, paper toweling, or newspaper in the bottom of the carrier. Start with short sessions of just a minute or two, and place your dragon inside the carrier with one of its favorite snacks. Leave the door open and stay right with your pet. If your dragon panics, don't force the issue. Let him come out of the carrier and give him time to calm down. Try again in an hour or so. As your dragon relaxes in the carrier, training sessions can last longer and you can practice with the door shut. As your dragon learns to associate the carrier with tasty food, he'll look forward to climbing in and staying put.

Be sure to label your carrier with pertinent information. Each of our dragon carriers has a large, highly visible luggage tag secured to the carrying handle with our name, address, and phone number. In addition, we've printed in large letters using indelible marker on both sides of the carrier our phone number and the words *HARMLESS REPTILES.*

Most reptiles hate to be moved. New surroundings frighten them, and they typically hide, refusing to eat, drink, or explore. Pet bearded dragons, however, seem to be less stressed than other reptiles by travel and new scenery.

We'll always remember one puny dragon recovering too slowly from a major injury. We decided to bring her along on an auto trip from the wintry north to warm, sunny Florida. Once in the Sunshine State, she basked, ate, and began her recovery because of the stimulation of bright sun and warm temperatures. So, while we recommend that other reptiles stay at home, we understand and appreciate families that won't leave their dragon behind when taking a vacation trip.

Travel Tips

Here are a few points to remember when traveling with dragons:

- ❏ Dragons overheat and die if left in a closed car on a warm or sunny day.

- ❏ Call ahead if you plan to travel by air. Many airlines won't allow reptiles in the cabin at any time or reptiles in cargo during hot weather. If your dragon does travel in cargo, special packing and insulation are essential. Don't try to sneak onto the plane with your dragon. While we can't say that we're innocent of such transgressions, we can say from experience that you should avoid the temptation.

- ❏ Bring food and especially water from home. Strange smells can inhibit a dragon from consuming different foods and water. You may wish to bring along your dragon's usual dishes for food and water.

- ❏ Plan on changing the carrier's bedding daily. Bring extra toweling.

- ❏ Remember that some people are afraid of reptiles. Don't frighten people with your dragon.

- ❏ Don't inadvertently frighten hotel housekeeping staff with your dragon. When traveling with our dragons, we request that our room not be serviced (and pick up fresh towels as needed from housekeeping) and leave a "Do Not Disturb" sign on the door.

- ❏ Hotel rooms, rugs, and bathtubs may have been treated with chemicals and insecticides. Be careful if you wish to let your dragon wander the room.

- ❏ Lawns and foliage growing at rest stops, golf courses, city parks, and suburban yards are likely to have been treated with chemicals. Be extremely careful when exposing your reptile to new areas.

  We must repeat once more: Your dragon will overheat and die if left in a closed car on a warm or sunny day. Be extra careful when traveling with your dragon.

Emergency Planning for Dragons

As much as we may try to avoid it, disaster can strike. The type of disaster varies widely, but we can almost guarantee that at some point you will confront an emergency that could potentially harm or kill yourself and your dragon.

Depending on the part of the country you live in, you may be vulnerable to earthquakes, blizzards, hurricanes, ice storms, tornadoes, floods, or fire. When there's a bearded dragon in the family, disaster preparedness includes planning for your dragon's welfare.

To begin, plan how your dragon would survive for a week or so if you could not leave your home. We're fortunate that dragons are omnivorous: they can survive on salads and snacks when live prey are unavailable. Owners have fed their dragons everything from granola to dry dog/cat food to thawed veggies and meats during times of emergency. Dragons can also survive several days of fasting, but they need water every day or so. Stock a few extra gallons of bottled water, so your dragon has a supply of fresh water for drinking and soaking.

Next, consider what to do if ordered to evacuate. Generally, there are two types of plans that should be made—how to evacuate with your dragon, and how to leave your dragon behind when you evacuate. Most emergency shelters accept only people, not pets. *Always* put the safety and survival of yourself and other humans ahead of your dragon. When there's an emergency, *never* risk your safety, even if it means leaving your dragon behind.

We learned the value of planning ahead when our power was out for five days after an ice storm, and for another five days after a hurricane. The most powerful lesson came with the realization that stress levels run high during emergencies and disasters, and that one's primary focus is the welfare of family and neighbors, and of saving one's life and property. When an emergency hits, you won't have time to begin thinking about your bearded dragon. Plan now.

Points to Consider in Planning:

❏ Keep a plastic cat carrier handy for transporting and housing (temporarily) your dragon.

❏ Keep a list of simple instructions for feeding and watering your dragon, along with its needs for light and heat. Post a set by a door to the house (we keep ours on a wall in the back porch) and by the dragon's enclosure. Keep these notes simple so they can be used by neighbors or disaster personnel if you can't get home because of an emergency.

❏ If you evacuate, post a note in indelible ink by the door most frequently used and in a location that will be seen by emergency personnel entering your house. Provide your name, where you can be found, and contact numbers for friends or family who are likely to know your whereabouts. If your dragon is in the house, state its location and emphasize that it is a *harmless* reptile.

❏ Keep with you the phone numbers of your veterinarian, reptile-keeping friends, and the local herp society or zoo. Remember, though, that everyone else is also dealing with the disaster and may be unable to help you. Also take along phone numbers for your insurance agent, your attorney, and those of the police, fire, and the Red Cross.

❏ If your dragon is likely to be chilled because of power outages or living in a motel or shelter, don't feed it. Wait until you can warm the lizard.

❏ Your dragon may need a veterinary checkup when the emergency ends, especially if it has been exposed to cold temperatures, smoke, fouled water, dehydration, or long periods of fasting. Dragons are hardy souls, but they'll appreciate pampering after surviving a disaster.

There's one more emergency that deserves special mention. A friend of ours who knew all of the inherent risks died in a house fire when he tried to save his pets. If your house catches on fire, get out! Don't stop for your dragon. Don't think you'll have time or luck. Get out immediately.

Saying Good-Bye

Someday, you and your dragon may part ways. You may lose interest in the lizard or be dealing with circumstances that demand placement of your pet in another home. We've dealt with this issue as dragon breeders, and our experiences may help you during these tough times. Here is some advice if you can no longer care for your dragon:

❏ Never turn your dragon loose. It will not survive for long, and the time spent until its death will be filled with terror and pain. Your dragon is no longer a wild animal and cannot fend for itself, whether in the city, suburbs, country, park, or wilderness area.

❏ Phone the closest zoo and herp societies. They often know of those who place unwanted reptiles into good homes.

❏ You may wish to advertise your dragon for sale in a local newspaper or bulletin board. Be sure to interview prospective buyers, and select the one you think will give your dragon a loving home and good care.

❏ We like to give our extra dragons to others, especially adolescents who have a burgeoning interest in reptiles, along with ample instructions on caring for their new pets. It's a way of giving back to herpetoculture, providing us with gratification and starting a new dragon owner on the right path. It might be right for you, too.

Sometimes even more difficult decisions must be made. Your dragon may be seriously ill, or very old. Helping a beloved pet to die humanely with minimal pain, stress, or fear is part of responsible ownership and the last gift that you can give your dragon. Here are some pointers:

❏ Never try to induce death in your dragon by putting it in the freezer or by withholding food and water. These practices are inhumane and will cause your dragon much pain and suffering.

❏ Consult with your veterinarian. Humane euthanasia is inexpensive and causes minimal suffering. Your veterinarian may offer advice as to the value of a necropsy (animal autopsy) and services such as cremation. If you wish, you can return home with your dragon's body for burial, receive its ashes for later burial, or let the vet dispose of the body. Don't throw the body out in the trash.

❏ Owners of pets that die go through a grieving process similar to that which occurs when a human friend or family member is lost. There are pet grief counselors and hot lines that can help. In time, you'll remember just the joy of owning a dragon, and we hope you'll consider once again opening your heart and home to another baby bearded dragon.

CHAPTER 7:

BEARDED DRAGON BEHAVIORS

Compared to many lizards, inland bearded dragons display a wide range of social behaviors. For obvious reasons, they will only display the full range of these behaviors once they reach sexual maturity and if they are kept in a group. Following are some of the behaviors you will notice in this species.

Social Hierarchies

In the wild or in captivity, bearded dragons raised in a group form social hierarchies relatively early in life. Using the terminology of animal behavior, the leader of any group is called the alpha animal.

If you raise a group of baby bearded dragons it quickly becomes apparent that some individuals are "top dogs," while others are submissive. During the immature stages, a clear distinction is usually seen between several of the more dominant individuals (rather than one alpha animal) and the more submissive dragons. The dominant dragons are more vigorous in their feeding behaviors and intimidate smaller, more submissive animals. As a pattern, bearded dragons that are aggressive feeders grow faster, which makes them need to eat more, which makes them more aggressive feeders, grabbing increasing portions of the food offered. Over time, intimidated smaller animals wisely become wary of the quick and daring feeding behaviors of larger ones, and thus have less access to food. They end up eating less and remaining smaller unless moved to separate rearing containers. Dominant juvenile bearded dragons, if hungry and underfed, often turn to

mutilating the tail tips, digits, and even lower limbs of less dominant animals. Larger immature bearded dragons may also attempt to eat smaller ones. In the world of bearded dragons, the first months of life are a ruthless race to feed and reach large size.

Once bearded dragons mature, their new reproduction-related behaviors kick in. Social hierarchies become more defined with a large male becoming the alpha animal of the group.

Climbing and Basking Site Hierarchies

Inland bearded dragons are considered semi-arboreal animals and will readily climb shrubs, rock piles, and fallen tree trunks when available. These raised structures often form the topographical nucleus of a group of bearded dragons.

In the wild and in well-designed greenhouse enclosures, bearded dragons compete for prime basking areas, usually the highest and most easily accessible sites such as fence posts, fallen trees, shrubs (such as the tops of large jade plants), or rock outcrops. Typically, the alpha male of a group acquires the top position on a basking site.

Thermoregulation

Like most reptiles, bearded dragons can raise their body temperature relatively quickly, but they cool down slowly, and cannot readily cool below air temperature. The preferred daytime body temperature of bearded dragons is around 98° F, which they can easily achieve by basking in sunlight even at air temperatures 10 or more degrees cooler than the target body temperature.

Bearded Dragons flatten and darken their bodies to increase heat absorption and quickly raise body temperature when exposed to sunlight. Bearded dragons can also warm their bodies by absorbing radiant heat from warm surfaces such as rocks or the ground. In the wild, as midday air temperatures rise toward 103° F, bearded dragons usually remain hidden and sheltered from the sun because they have a limited ability to cool below air temperature. That is the reason it is very important that a basking site in a vivarium be offset by a cooler section. We have had several reports of bearded dragons that are heated day and night with one or more spotlights and heat strips running the length of a vivarium gaping for extended periods of time, that are hyperactive and obviously heat stressed, who sud-

The baby bearded dragon basking under a spotlight is gaping to dissipate heat.

denly die. The importance of a cooler sheltered area in the upper 70s to low 80s during the day cannot be emphasized enough.

Gaping or Panting When Basking

Some bearded dragons choose to remain at high temperatures and may gape (keep the mouth open) or pant (keep the mouth open while performing throat movements to increase the rate of air flow in and out of the mouth and lungs) while basking. Gaping is also performed in the initial stages of overheating, presumably in an attempt to cool down. This behavior should not be of concern to owners unless their vivarium is overheated and fails to provide cool areas. If the enclosure is too hot, heat sources should be turned off and the vivarium design adjusted to provide a heat gradient. Gaping and forced exhalation may also occur in bearded dragons with respiratory infections, with lung damage from inhaling too much dust, or with certain types of parasite infection. Clearly, interpreting the cause of gaping must be made in the context of husbandry, often with a veterinarian's help.

This eastern bearded dragon is extending its beard. Photo by David Travis.

Open-Mouth Bearded Display

Bearded dragon hatchlings perform the classic display of an open mouth with beard extended toward large moving objects they interpret as threats. It's easy to see how this defensive display earned these lizards their common name. In captivity, most bearded dragons readily habituate to movements by their caretakers and the propensity to perform the open-mouth display quickly wanes. Nonetheless, the potential to perform this display remains throughout the life of a bearded dragon. The eastern bearded dragon tends to perform this display much more readily than inland bearded dragons and is not as likely to habituate to large moving objects. However, any suddenly startled individual may perform a bearded display *(left)*, and individuals who are considered aggressive do so even more readily. Higher temperatures in the 90s will usually increase the likelihood of a bearded dragon performing a bearded display. No matter how habituated a bearded dragon may become to humans, suddenly exposing bearded dragons to certain animals such as snakes and monitors seems to readily elicit the display and is a trick resorted to by herp photographers.

Mutilation/Cannibalism

Juveniles of all the popular species may mutilate cage mates. This behavior is most readily performed by stage 2 animals, usually by larger individuals toward more passive ones when not enough food is available. Tail tips, toes, and sections of limbs may be bitten off by hungry and more assertive individuals. In extreme cases, when a smaller dragon is of gobbling size, larger, more dominant juveniles may attempt cannibalism.

Until recently, we had not witnessed mutilation in subadult or adult bearded dragons. Specific conditions, however, did result in a significant level of mutilation incidence (eight subadults and two young adults were mutilated within a week) in a large breeding facility. Three factors were identified as contributing to mutilation: limited food availability, overcrowdedness, and high temperatures

(90–105°F). Large adults seldom mutilate other dragons of similar size. Close observation of bearded dragons usually reveals that when mutilation does occur in subadults, it is often one individual doing the damage in a group. Within a group, if the conditions leading to mutilation persist, the end result is often a single able and actively feeding individual and several feeding handicapped and crippled dragons.

Arm-Waving

Arm-waving is the earliest social behavior in bearded dragons and it can be witnessed within days of hatching. It serves both as an intraspecies signal (basically, "I'm a bearded dragon.") and as an appeasement gesture ("Please don't hurt me."). It persists as an appeasement/submissive gesture in adult females during breeding. More rarely it is performed by submissive males when more aggressive males bite their necks.

Tail Curling

Bearded dragons commonly adopt a position in which most of the tail is curled up above the ground as they remain still. This is a sign of being on alert and is com-

monly performed by adult bearded dragons throughout the day.

Head-Bobbing or Head-Jerking

Head-bobbing refers to a lowering and quick raising of the dragon's head, usually performed in repetitive sets. The lifting component of the behavior can be so vigorous that the entire front of the body jerks upward. This behavior (called head-jerking by some) is most often seen when males are in breeding/territorial mode, usually exhibiting a black beard. This is a sexual display performed as a part of courtship toward females prior to copulation.

Male-Male Encounters

At the onset of the breeding season, male-to-male encounters and occasional male-male fights occur. These fights are mostly ritualistic and no serious harm comes of them. Typically two males in breeding condition will blacken their beards and perform head-bobbing behaviors. This will be followed by a great bluff performance in which males tilt their flattened bodies toward each other. One of the males may twitch its tail. A male may then try to bite the tail of the other. They may bob and again display flat-

tened bodies to each other. A male may then decide to latch on to the thick ridge of scales around the neck in a movement that resembles breeding, pressing its body on top of the submissive animal. The beaten male flattens on the ground. These behaviors help select for fitness in bearded dragons, allowing the largest, strongest, healthiest, and most spirited males first access to available females.

Tongue-Tasting

Dragons taste new foods, new objects, and other dragons with their tongues. Tongue-tasting serves a chemoreceptive function and allows evaluation and identification of food, objects, or other lizards. Tongue-tasting may also be performed by alpha males upon other males prior to performing the head-bobbing display.

CHAPTER 8:
BREEDING BEARDED DRAGONS

Strategies for Breeding Bearded Dragons

Many people have set out to become rich breeding bearded dragons, hoping to meet the high demand for one of America's most popular pet lizards. Today most of them are out of business. They lasted only a couple of years because their projects lost money or were barely profitable. Indoor space and setup, electricity, food, and maintenance costs can be surprisingly high when keeping large numbers of bearded dragons indoors. In warmer areas, outdoor setups such as greenhouses are more economical but can bring other problems such as fire ants and inclement or unpredictable weather. As anyone who has made a living breeding amphibians and reptiles will tell you, it has to be a labor of love because it takes a great deal of work to make it

This greenhouse breeding setup has individual pens on one side and baby-rearing enclosures on the other. Greenhouses reduce electrical costs in commercial bearded dragon breeding operations.

In this outdoor commercial breeding operation, the dragon pens have smooth fiberglass walls that prevent escape and can be covered with shade or plastic as needed.

in what many consider to be a cutthroat business. To be successful as a commercial breeder means doing research on the market, finding ready outlets for your animals, maintaining careful records of your breeding stock's performance and carefully planning the expenses and expected returns.

Herpetoculture is a very competitive and fast-changing business. What is popular today may not be marketable a few years from now, and what is rare today can become tomorrow's standard pet-trade fare, bred by every pet owner who cares to keep a pair together. To survive on a commercial level means constantly evaluating the market, the state and efficiency of your business, and your breeding stock. Ideally, you should always be looking to produce more vigorous, as well as more beautiful, dragons as economically as possible.

Record Keeping

A key to the success of any commercial breeder is record keeping. This means, at the very least, giving each animal a number, recording the parents of a particular clutch, the number of eggs laid by a female, and the number of eggs successfully hatched. Keeping digital photographic records

of individuals, labeled with their record number, can also allow you to keep digital files in a computer that can be readily accessed when planning breeding projects. It saves time and allows a broader overview than examining individual animals in a collection.

Egg clutches should be labeled with their parentage and the date laid. Records should also be maintained on incubation temperature and duration. Often dragons are good producers for about three years before the numbers produced start declining significantly. Thus, replacing commercial breeding stock is an important way to optimize production. This also means planning ahead to raise replacement stock. If your goal is to develop your own unique lines or to maintain existing lines, careful record keeping will prove invaluable in identifying the best individuals for the process. Expenses and sales should also be carefully recorded for tax purposes and for allowing you to hone the efficiency of your business.

Many breeders have lines of red/gold dragons crossed with Sandfire bearded dragons. The results combine characteristics of both morphs.

Selective Breeding

Selective breeding is a term that refers to crossing animals with desirable traits to establish particular characteristics (such as color) in a line while maintaining vigor (size,

Damaged limbs from intraspecies mutilation in subadult bearded dragons do not grow back, and injured animals are permanently handicapped.

health, and reproductive ability). Most of the attractive bearded dragon morphs available today were developed in this manner. Although inbreeding (breeding animals that are closely related, such as brother x sister or father x daughter) is a common and necessary component of selective breeding, it can decrease line vigor if practiced extensively over several generations. For this reason, selective breeding must also include outcrossing in order to reintroduce vigor from an unrelated gene pool while retaining the desirable trait.

Outcrossing

The opposite of inbreeding, outcrossing consists of breeding animals that have desirable traits with unrelated animals. It is done to maintain line vigor or to add additional characteristics to a line. For example, German giants have been crossed with other lines of bearded dragons to increase size, reproductive vigor, and fecundity. Although first generation offspring from an outbreeding may bear little resemblance to the bright-colored parent, crossing these outbred first generation animals together will usually result in a percentage that manifest the desirable traits. Selective breeding can then be used to "fix" or intensify these traits.

Breeding Requirements

The first requirement for breeding bearded dragons is to have at least one healthy young adult male and one healthy young adult female. The second is to keep them together. The third requirement, usually after the first breeding season, is to allow them a winter shutdown or rest period. When they're mature they will tend to brumate no matter what you do. In captivity, breeding starts after winter shutdown is over, beginning in the spring and often continuing into fall.

Many keepers claim they have their best breeding success when they keep bearded dragons in individual pairs, and this may be true when they're kept in small indoor enclosures. In our experience, it is possible to keep trios, one male and two females, with good breeding results. For commercial breeders, the expense of maintaining any more males than necessary can become cost prohibitive. In larger enclosures, 72 x 30 inches minimum, we keep ratios of two males and four females and have found this to be the most effective ratio for commercial-scale breeding.

Breeding Patterns

With bearded dragons raised under intensive rearing conditions, breeding begins by as early as five to six months of age and can extend through the first winter. By twelve months of age, bearded dragons raised under intensive conditions may produce up to three clutches of eggs. During the course of their second year (twelve to twenty-four months) they can lay up to seven clutches of eggs (two to three clutches before the first winter shutdown and four to five clutches after winter shutdown).

Under less-intensive rearing conditions in outdoor greenhouses and given a first year winter shutdown, sexual maturity may not be reached until bearded dragons are twelve to fifteen months old. Three clutches will be produced in the first eighteen months of age and after the second (greenhouse conditions) winter shutdown up to seven clutches for typical bearded dragons. The third year, only three to four clutches will be produced.

In this green-house operation, dragons are housed in large plastic bins. Panels of polyurethane foam are used for shade.

This is a pattern we have seen in several other species of quickly maturing lizards with high reproductive rates. The females are prolific breeders for the first two to three years and then steadily decline in production. By six years, egg production is insignificant, and by seven years, it has often ceased completely. One important lesson is that from the point of view of a commercial breeder, buying large adult captive-raised females is usually not the best investment. One-year-old animals are probably the best buy for breeders.

Prebreeding Conditioning and Winter Shutdown

In captivity, beginning with their second winter, most bearded dragons undergo a period of winter shutdown. During this time, they become inactive, spending extended periods of time in shelters and eating little or no food. This period of brumation appears necessary for long-term success in breeding bearded dragons.

As a rule, most mature bearded dragons shut down on their own, no matter what conditions they're kept in, but a shift in environmental conditions also plays a role in initiating brumation. In outdoor or greenhouse conditions, the reduction of the daily duration of light exposure and dropping temperatures naturally induce brumation. In the home, starting in the first two weeks of December (in the Northern Hemisphere), light exposure should be reduced to ten hours a day (adjust the timer) and spotlights replaced with lower-wattage bulbs so that the temperature at basking sites is 75–80°F. In addition, all secondary heat sources such as hot rocks should be turned off, and night temperatures should drop into the 60s. In most homes, one way to achieve cooler night temperatures is to keep bearded dragons in tanks at floor level. This winter shut-down regime is maintained for about two months, starting sometime in December and ending in February. After this period, vivarium conditions should be returned to a normal regime.

Visual Perspectives and Breeding

FAQ: *I have a pair of inland bearded dragons that I purchased two years ago and I have yet to see signs of breeding. They are in a 36-inch-long enclosure with a small one-tube fluorescent fixture and an incandescent bulb. What am I doing wrong?*

We were surprised to hear of people failing to breed their bearded dragons, considering these lizards are among the easiest reptiles to breed. Surprisingly we have received several of these reports and we attribute these failures to improper husbandry. Remember that bearded dragons are diurnal and depend on visual clues to elicit breeding behaviors. A common cause of breeding failure is too small of an enclosure. Bearded dragons benefit from the greater range of visual perspectives and social behaviors possible in larger enclosures. Another cause may be inadequate lighting. Animals kept in setups with low levels of lights may also fail to breed. A simple method for getting bearded dragons to breed was discovered by a well-known bearded dragon expert. Remove the dragons from their cage and place them on the floor of a room in an area lit by a spotlight. Within minutes the male will usually head bob and attempt to breed the female. If she is receptive, you will usually end up with a clutch of fertile eggs.

Copulation

About three to four weeks after the end of winter shut-down, bearded dragons begin reproductive activities, including courtship, territorial and competitive behaviors, and copulation. In bearded dragons, copulation is typical of what is observed for most lizards. A male bites the fleshy portion of a female's nape, places part of his upper body on her, then scratches her with his hind leg to encourage her to position herself for copulation. The male then twists his lower body and inserts a hemipenis. The sexual act lasts several minutes.

Gestation

Gestation, the period between copulation and egg-laying, can be difficult to accurately determine in reptiles because females of many species can store sperm for extended periods of time. As a rule for bearded dragons, the interval between a first breeding and egg-laying will be about four to six weeks. Subsequently the interval between clutches during a breeding season can vary depending on a number of factors and be as short as three weeks or considerably longer.

Egg-Laying

As the gestation period nears its end, the eggs pass through an area of the oviduct surrounded by the shell gland, which forms the calcareous shell. After they pass through the shell gland, you can often see the outlines of individual eggs (now more rigidly enclosed) pressing against the abdominal wall. They look like grapes or marbles. Shortly after, the lizard displays behaviors such as investigating possible laying sites and digging several test burrows.

At this time, it is important to provide the pregnant (or gravid) female with a nest site of at least 12 inches of burrowing substrate. Most breeders provide damp soil as substrate. If the substrate is too shallow or causes repeated collapse of a burrow, the female may refuse to dig a nest and instead lay an egg a day on the surface until she finds a suitable laying site. (This presents a problem because uncovered eggs have a high rate of dehydration and may be harmed by exposure to excess heat or sunlight.) Or, she may dig several test holes and lay scattered eggs on the surface. She may eventually lay the rest of her eggs in shallow soil, but instead of digging her preferred nest (one deep enough that she can completely fit into, with the tip of her snout at the nest hole) she may lay them with the front of her body exposed.

An accessible 5-gallon plastic flower pot filled with moistened potting soil generally works well as a nesting site. After introducing the damp soil, compress it by pressing down on the soil surface with your hand. This makes the soil less likely to collapse as the female digs her nest. Alternatively, nesting sites can be made by placing soil at least 12 inches deep at one end of the primary enclosure. Also, the female can be placed in a 30- or 55-gallon trashcan with a least 12 inches of soil in the bottom. Gently press down the moistened soil before introducing the female into the container. Substrate moisture is believed to provide important egg-laying cues regarding the suitability of the laying medium. Our records show that most female bearded dragons lay their eggs between 1 P.M. and 6 P.M.

Only the tip of the female's snout can be seen at the entrance to the burrow when she lays her eggs.

Clutch Size

In our inland bearded dragon collections, clutch sizes have ranged from as few as seven to as many as forty-six eggs, with most clutches ranging between twenty and thirty eggs. The German giant line of bearded dragons has been reported to lay in excess of fifty eggs per clutch, with a record of sixty-eight eggs. Clutch size varies depending on size, age, morph, and line of the parents. As a rule, younger,

Carefully move eggs from the nest to an incubator.

smaller females lay smaller clutches and old females eventually lay smaller and fewer clutches. Numbers of clutches can also vary from as few as one in first-year breeders to as many as seven in second- to third-year breeders.

Incubation

After your dragon lays her eggs, carefully dig through the soil using your fingers or a tablespoon to expose the egg clutch. Then transfer the eggs to an incubation container such as a plastic storage box or an incubator containing 1 1/2 inches of incubating medium. The media most commonly used by breeders are coarse vermiculite, perlite, and a 50:50 mix of perlite and vermiculite. We currently use only perlite as an incubating medium for bearded dragon eggs. We add water to the medium until it feels moist but not soggy, until it barely clumps when held in the hand but does not drip water if squeezed. (This is about 4 parts incubating medium to 3 parts water by weight, not volume.) We expose part of the eggs to allow for monitoring. We half bury eggs horizontally in the medium, leaving a small space between each egg. If you are using plastic containers as incubators, you should use a cover and place three pinholes (use a heated nail held in pliers, or a fine

drill) in the top, leaving at least 1 1/2 inches of air space between the top and the eggs.

The ideal incubation temperature for bearded dragons is 82–85°F. To provide this, most small-scale breeders use inexpensive poultry incubators such as the Hovabator. Large-scale breeders construct heated cabinets using either lightbulbs or heat tape controlled by a thermostat. Careful calibration is critical to prevent overheating. Temperatures that are too warm (above 89°F) will result in the death of the embryo as will temperatures that are too cool (long-term at less than 75°F or short-term at cold temps, such as low 60s and below). Another important step is to check for hot and cool spots in the incubator. A thermometer and thermostatic control are essential to good monitoring.

It is also important to monitor moisture content in the incubation substrate. Most breeders do this by picking up a clump of substrate, rolling it between the fingers and pressing it into a ball. If the substrate still feels damp, it is probably fine. If it feels almost dry, then the substrate surface should be misted lightly. Substrate can be checked weekly, but if it is found to be too dry, check daily for a while and mist as necessary.

Humidity within the incubator can be monitored as

well. For a simple incubator (such as a Hovabator) with substrate placed directly on its floor, adding a small container of water helps to maintain appropriate humidity levels. If using a thermostatically controlled incubator, there should be little condensation on its sides. However, if you are incubating eggs in a room with fluctuating day/night temperatures, there can be considerable condensation. Usually this is not a problem if the substrate is appropriately moist. Adding ventilation holes to the sides of the egg container can reduce condensation but will hasten the rate of substrate drying as well.

Incubation time varies depending on species. *Pogona vitticeps* eggs range from fifty-five to seventy-five days depending on temperature. Lawson's dragon *(P. henrylawsoni)* eggs will hatch in forty-five to fifty-five days, and eastern bearded dragon *(P. barbata)* eggs hatch in sixty-nine to seventy-nine days. With most clutches, all eggs will hatch within twenty-four hours of the first hatching, but in some, the clutch may take as long as six days.

Setting Incubator Temperatures
The process of properly calibrating an incubator temperature can require several hours with homemade incubators or inexpensive poultry incubators. We recommend that an incubator be properly calibrated at least twelve hours before the eggs are introduced. To calibrate an incubator, adjust the thermostat so that the temperature inside the incubator matches the desired setting. To get a temperature reading inside the incubator, place a mercury thermometer inside so it is visible through a window, or install a digital thermometer with an external probe. Placing the probe inside the incubator and setting the switch to out/probe will give you a continuous readout as you adjust the thermostat. Because it takes time for the air temperature to equilibrate inside the incubator, several thermostatic adjustments will be required over a few hours for accurate calibration.

Note: It is important to keep the incubator in a room cooler than the desired incubation temperature, particularly during summer heat waves. Remember that inexpensive incubators heat but do not cool, so they cannot lower the incubator temperature below ambient air temperature. Also, take into consideration that brief exposure to high temperatures (above 90°F) is more likely to kill a developing embryo than brief exposure to cool temperatures

Temperature-Dependent Sex Determination in Bearded Dragons

FAQ: *Based on the sex ratios of bearded dragons hatched in my collection, it appears that incubation temperature could play a role in determining the sex of bearded dragons. Do you think it's possible?*

Temperature dependent sex determination (TDSD) is a complex subject best resolved by genetic research and experimentation. The only possible answer we can give at this time is that there are indications that there may be TDSD in bearded dragons. In the last couple of years, clutches that we have incubated at 82–84°F have yielded a higher proportion of males than in previous years when eggs were incubated at 84–86°F. One breeder told us that a clutch he incubated at 82°F yielded mostly males. Other breeders of frilled dragons have reported that they have had a high male ratio when eggs were incubated at a steady 84–85°F. Temperature dependent sex determination in bearded dragons has yet to be fully understood but will likely be clarified by additional data from breeders who keep careful records of incubation temperatures and monitor hatchlings until their sex can definitely be determined.

Turning Eggs

Many herpetoculturists correctly warn against turning reptile eggs in the later stages of development. Lizard eggs begin to develop from the moment of fertilization so development is usually well on its way by the time the clutch is laid. At a certain stage in its development, the embryo forms an allantois, a membranous outgrowth from the midgut. This eventually expands and fuses with one of the membranes that encloses the embryo, called the chorion, to form the chorio-allantoic membrane, an area that allows gas exchange through the overlying shell. Typically, the chorio-allantoic membrane forms at the top section of a resting egg with the back of the embryo curved beneath the allantois. Thus, in incubating eggs, the approx-

imate position of the developing embryo is toward the top, close to where gas exchange readily occurs. Turning the egg in the later stages of development will shift the gas exchange area and can cause compression, which, depending on the egg position, may suffocate the embryo. So, the general rule is to avoid turning eggs once they have been placed in an incubator.

To keep a record of the original placement of eggs, draw an X on top of each egg with a soft-lead pencil. In case of accidents or late discovery of eggs, the eggs can also be "candled" to determine the embryo position. To do this, place a bright light behind a pinhole in a sheet of cardboard, and view each egg with the light shining through it. The developing embryo will appear as a dark mass. Place the egg in the incubator so that the dark mass appears at the top.

Hatch Failure

Several factors can prevent eggs from hatching. When eggs show signs that they are going bad, the timing can indicate probable causes. First check incubation parameters such as substrate moisture and temperature. If eggs incubated under proper conditions show early signs of collapse or molding, infertility (eggs aren't fertilized) is often the cause. This can be verified by slitting the collapsed eggs and checking for signs of early embryonic development and blood vessels. Other factors that can cause the early demise of embryos include genetics and disease.

Late stage death can be caused by genetic factors, improper temperatures or moisture levels, and possibly by faulty yolk composition. Work we have done with other species suggests that if incubation temperature is too high there can come a point when increased metabolism and higher oxygen requirements of late-stage embryos may exceed the amount of oxygen diffusing through the shell. At the first signs of late-stage egg death (collapse and no hatching by thirty-six hours) we check temperature and lower it a few degrees.

Another cause of egg hatching failure may be linked to temperatures that are too low and extend incubation for too long. Much to our surprise, some lizard eggs incubated at relatively cool temperatures showed near-term hatchlings with soft bones and rubbery snouts and legs—signs of metabolic bone disease. Our current hypothesis is that incubation periods that extend too long can sometimes result in large hatchlings with depleted calcium reserves. Finally, it has been hypothesized that yolk compositions can be directly affected by diet and supplements fed to the female, resulting in inadequate or excessive amounts of certain nutrients. These deficiencies or excesses may harm developing embryos, and this is a topic that deserves further study.

In many areas, carrion flies may infest bearded dragon eggs. These annoying pests take advantage of any deterioration or rupture of the shell to feed on the egg contents and lay their eggs. They are readily attracted to the smell of eggs that have gone bad, which is one reason you should remove these eggs as soon as they are noticed. Otherwise, carrion flies will lay their eggs in rotting dragon eggs, and before long your incubator will be infested with hundreds of these flies. If many carrion flies are in your incubator or

This clutch of bearded dragons is hatching.

the surrounding area, they will wait like predators for any opportunity to feed on animal matter, including a baby bearded dragon that has just slit its shell. In most cases, baby dragons will hatch before any real damage is done, but check for maggots in the umbilical area and in any remaining egg yolk. The maggots can be rinsed off with tap water.

Hatching

For twenty-four hours prior to hatching, bearded dragon eggs sweat to varying degrees; the sweating is followed by a slight collapse and noticeable loss of turgidity of the egg twelve hours prior to hatching. Healthy, vigorous animals usually slit through the egg shell (using an egg tooth at the tip of the snout) within a few hours of this initial collapse. After hatching, newborn dragons may still be coated with albumin and will remain within the egg for several hours. They should not be disturbed or removed from the incubation container until they have emerged from the eggs and show signs of activity. After the hatchlings are observed to be active, they can then be transferred to rearing containers.

Removing Bearded Dragons from Eggs That Fail to Hatch

FAQ: *I recently had a clutch of bearded dragon eggs. After noticing the initial collapse that precedes hatching, a number of babies hatched but several failed to slit the eggs. Could I have manually removed the babies?*

In our experience, manually removing babies from eggs results mostly in failure. At best, you can slit the eggs after twenty-four hours of the initial collapse, and hope.

To slit an unhatched egg, use cuticle scissors to penetrate the shell and cut close to the shell, making sure that you do not penetrate past the shell surface. The slit should run through the center third of the egg. Once the egg is slit, leave it alone. In time, a baby lizard may emerge on its own. Never manually pull a lizard out of the egg following incision. In our experience lizards that are manually removed usually die. In spite of these procedures, we have found that most lizards that fail to slit their eggs on their own, also fail to emerge from manually slit eggs. Of the few that do, most go on to die. In other words, the value of slitting unhatched eggs is questionable.

CHAPTER 9:
THE BOLD AND THE BEAUTIFUL: MORPHS

P art of the fun of owning reptiles is to experience the variants produced by breeding. Whether the animal has a special size or color, the variants are usually referred to as morphs. Perhaps nowhere are morphs more exciting and challenging than those in the bearded dragon world.

Inland bearded dragons have a wide distribution in Australia and consist of many populations adapted to specific habitats ranging from sandy deserts to savannas, mountains, and woodlands. The variation found in these wild populations has allowed herpetoculturists to produce the range of morphs currently established in captivity. According to Hauschild and Bosch (2000), the popular inland bearded dragons with high amounts of red originate from the central part of their range—an area characterized by red sands—while the more yellow specimens are found in the southern yellow sand deserts. The availability of these more colorful desert morphs in the early 1990s allowed the selective breeding of many colorful varieties of bearded dragons available today.

Morphs Recognized in the U.S.
Normal
These original brown and tan bearded dragons with small amounts of red and yellow, mostly on the head, were first imported into the U.S. in the late 1980s. "Normals" were the most readily available bearded dragons until the herpetocultural revolution generated imports of red/gold dragons in the 1990s. Because of the increased demand for

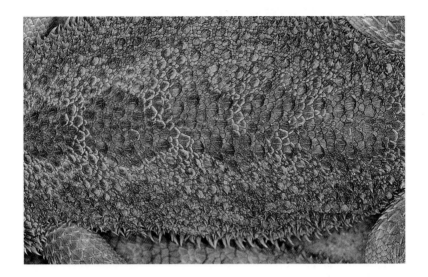

more colorful dragons, most normal dragons in captivity
have, over time, been crossed with red/golds to the degree
that it is becoming increasingly difficult to find representa-
tives of the once common normal strain. This is the same
herpetocultural pattern we are now seeing with leopard
geckos—selection for brighter colors and bolder patterns
causing a decline in the pet trade of the original, normal-
colored individuals.

Note the complex scalation in this close-up of a bearded dragon's back.

German Giant

Pete Weis introduced this morph into the U.S. hobby.
German giants are big dragons with a lot of spunk and are
generally prolific breeders. They are colored mostly in
browns and tans. The head is less massive than in typical
dragons. The iris is a silvery gold that contrasts sharply
with the pupil. Because of their high fecundity, German
giants have been crossed with other lines to increase
reproductive vigor. The giants, however, can be a little
more prone to aggressive behavior than are typical dragons. Large males sometimes exceed 24 inches in length,
and females can lay single clutches of more than fifty eggs,
with a record of sixty-eight eggs (Kevin Dunne, pers.
comm.).

German giant morph of the inland bearded dragon. Photo by Kevin Dunne.

Red/Gold

A great revolution in dragon breeding followed the importation of individuals with extensive amounts of reds, oranges, and varying amounts of yellow in the early 1990s. Originating in Germany, red/gold dragons allowed the selective breeding of the many orange, red, and yellow lines available today, including the Sandfire line. The original German breeding stock was said to have come from the red deserts of the interior of Australia. Additional imports of red/gold crosses between lines (e.g., normal x red/gold; and Sandfire x red /gold) and selective breeding have allowed various breeders to develop their own unique lines. Because yellow and red pigments are synthesized by skin cells called xanthophores, the term *xanthic* may be the most appropriate to describe lines characterized by varying degrees of red or yellow coloration. Red/golds could be considered the most basic examples of xanthism in bearded dragons.

Hyperxanthic

Extreme forms of xanthism, developed through selective

breeding for extensive saturation of red/orange or yellow, qualify as hyperxanthic. The first established hyperxanthic lines of bearded dragons were the Sandfire lines developed by author Robert Mailloux and characterized by bright orange to orange-red coloration distributed throughout the upper body and limbs to the point of masking most of the typical pattern seen on dragons.

The Sandfire line was started from a single unusually bright colored female of the red/gold morph with orange-red extending to the limbs. Selective breeding for increased saturation of the bright orange coloration established the Sandfire characteristics and this morph is now produced with regularity. The full expression of the hyperxanthic trait is dependent on the right light exposure. Sandfire bearded dragons raised under standard indoor conditions are more brightly colored than typical dragons, but they do not come close to the intense orange-reds of Sandfire animals raised outdoors or in sun-exposed greenhouses. One hypothesis is that the saturation with red/orange pigment is a dermal response to sunlight exposure, much like tanning in human skin.

In addition to the Sandfire lines, there are several other hyperxanthic lines, some of which may also include varying degrees of hypomelanism (reduced dark pigmentation) such as some of the yellow bearded dragons bred in the U.S. and in Europe. Yellow lines in general have proven difficult to establish, many showing poor reproductive vigor, poor hatch rate, or poor hatchling survival. Careful breeding and outbreeding may succeed in establishing a hardy yellow line in the not too distant future.

Tiger
This was a line first introduced by Ron Tremper and characterized by a barred pattern running the width of the body.

Striped
Although some juvenile bearded dragons have a striped pattern, this usually fades by the time they mature.

A high contrast red/gold x Sandfire cross

Young red/gold bearded drag-ons show early signs of red coloration.

Red/gold males can develop bright-ly colored heads that contrast sharply with their less col-orful bodies.

Red/gold crosses can be highly variable in appearance and are an important source of new morphs.

Top of the line Sandfire bearded dragons are solid orange and nearly pattern-less. This vivid coloration has only been achieved after three or more months of daily exposure to sunlight.

The Sandfire trait becomes apparent in subadults and intensifies as they grow to sexual maturity.

An older
female
Sandfire
bearded drag-
on

Close-up of the
skin of a
Sandfire
bearded drag-
on

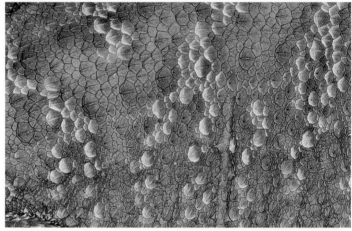

Sandfire yel-
low bearded
dragon

An outstanding example of a yellow bearded dragon produced by Dragon's Den Herpetoculture. Photo by Kevin Dunne

A yellow bearded dragon produced by Sandfire Dragon Ranch

A yellow line of the bearded dragon originally developed in England by Luke Yeomans. Photo by Jerry Cole

Juvenile tiger morph

Adult tiger morph bearded dragon

Various degrees of striping are seen in baby bearded dragons, and some dragons retain the stripes into adulthood.

Striped hyperxanthic bearded dragon

The Snow dragon is a hypomelanistic line produced by Dragon's Den Herpetoculture. Photo by Kevin Dunne

A fourteen-month-old hypomelanistic bearded dragon. Photo by Kevin Dunne

Gold iris morph bred by Robert Mailloux. Photo by Corey Blanc

Gold iris bearded dragon produced by Kevin Dunne. Photo by Kevin Dunne

Bearded dragon breeders are actively working on selecting and developing new morphs. This is an unusual form of Sandfire bearded dragon with lightly colored reticulations.

A Sandfire novelty with pink and purple highlights.

Notice the striking combination of pattern and color in this Sandfire novelty with pink and purple highlights

Pastel morph of the inland bearded dragon. This is a male hypomelanistic red/gold. Photo by David Travis

Nonetheless, some individuals retain pale stripes into adulthood, a trait that could be selected for.

Hypomelanistic

These are dragons in which the dark pigmentation (melanin) is greatly reduced or nearly absent. Although they're very bleached in appearance, they are not true albinos because their eyes remain pigmented (in true albinism eyes are pink or orange/red). One of the characteristics of hypomelanistic dragons is a clear-colored nail base. At least two lines have been developed. One is the Sandfire "Pastel" line developed by Robert Mailloux, which is characterized by high-contrast oranges against a pale background. Pastels can also have light bluish to purplish body patterns, probably caused by clear skin areas that expose underlying iridophores, which are skin pigment cells that underlie xanthophores and have the ability to reflect light of specific wavelength. Another popular hypomelanistic line is the Snow dragon line established by Kevin Dunne, owner of Dragon's Den. As the name indicates, top of the line Snow dragons are mostly bright white. The high contrast between the gold iris and the near white body of Snow dragons makes this a particularly appealing morph. Depending on their backgrounds, hypomelanistic dragons can range from nearly pure white lizards to whitish animals with grayish patterns. Others may have intense yellows, oranges, or reds against a pale background.

Leucistic

These are uniformly colored, gray-white dragons with dark irises and bluish eyelids. A small number of breeders are working to establish this unusual morph.

Green

There is at least one natural population of gray-green bearded dragons in Australia. In captivity a pale green line was developed through selective breeding in England, but it has been difficult to maintain.

Gold Iris

We have had a few specimens hatch with unusually light, bright silvery-gold irises that contrast sharply with a black pupil. Kevin Dunne of Dragon's Den has also reported hatching individuals with light-colored irises. This is an attractive trait that will likely be developed through selective breeding.

The Future

Bearded dragons are becoming one of the most popular pet reptiles of all time, so it should be no surprise that there is an active interest in developing new, attractive, and marketable lines of this species. As with certain kinds of fish, such as koi carp and goldfish, or with lizards such as the popular leopard gecko, we can expect the availability of many more attractive and unusual morphs of bearded dragons in the future.

An unusual green morph of *P. vitticeps* photographed in the wild by Robert Mailloux

CHAPTER 10:

DISEASES OF BEARDED DRAGONS AND THEIR TREATMENTS

text and photos by Roger Klingenberg, D.V.M.

When bearded dragons were introduced as a new type of reptile pet several years ago, it appeared that we had found a truly bullet-proof lizard. Bearded dragons were hardy, good eaters, and easy to care for. Health problems were rare, and most disorders were chalked up to glitches in evolving husbandry techniques. As always happens with new reptiles, our knowledge base of the bearded dragon expanded exponentially as the species became more popular.

We have recently found that bearded dragons are not bulletproof, and while quite hardy, these lizards are afflicted by various ailments. Our medical and surgical knowledge of bearded dragons is increasing, but customer demand is what drives the evolution of new medical information and techniques. Much of what is medically applied to the bearded dragon is information we have borrowed from our work on the green iguana. We need more species-specific information, which is where you, the bearded dragon owner, can help. Participation and contribution to research at your local herpetological society or with the Association of Reptile and Amphibian Veterinarians is critical for the development of new medical information and techniques.

Recognizing Sick Bearded Dragons

One reason bearded dragons have become so popular is that they are personable and animated. Unlike certain snakes that spend a considerable amount of time wrapped up and vegetating contentedly, bearded dragons are active and entertaining. Each dragon has a unique personality and unique behavioral patterns, which are important for owners to evaluate during their normal caretaking duties. Simply put, sick children look sick, sick dogs look sick, sick cats look sick, and sick bearded dragons *look* and *act* sick. If, as an owner of a bearded dragon, you have missed the foot-stomping, arm-waving, tail-swishing, head-bobbing, sideways head tilts, and various other gymnastic techniques that bearded dragons use to communicate their feelings, resolve to watch more carefully in the future.

The most common signs of a sick bearded dragon are listlessness, inactivity, lying flat (instead of raising the body when standing), failing to eat or drink, and lack of normal communicative body language. In short, they are depressed and won't eat. Do any of these actions, or the lack thereof, indicate a particular disease or ailment? Unfortunately, they do not. These symptoms can be noted

A healthy lizard is curious, alert, active, and hungry. When stimulated, it stands up on its front feet, lifting its entire underside off the ground.

in all of the serious yet common bearded dragon ailments discussed here.

Parasites

Coccidiosis

Coccidiosis is the most common disorder seen in bearded dragons. Coccidia are microscopic, protozoan parasites that live primarily in the small intestine and replicate in the lining cells of the intestinal tract. The end product of the reproductive process is a microscopic entity called an oocyst. These tiny oocysts are passed into the environment with the feces when the bearded dragon has a bowel movement. The oocysts can then reinfect the host by being ingested. If your bearded dragon is anything like Lily, my daughter's bearded dragon, this happens frequently. Lily stomps through her waste as if it were put there for her entertainment. She then proceeds to stomp through her water dish and veggies, potentially contaminating the food and water with oocysts as she goes. Crickets and mealworms loose in the cage also crawl through or munch on the evacuated bowel materials. The crowning moment is when Lily takes a little nibble at her own stools, which is not an abnormal behavior. This is a direct life cycle at work; no intermediate hosts are required. One coccidium becomes a dozen, twelve coccidia become hundreds, and so on.

Coccidia are so prevalent in bearded dragons that they have their own species of coccidia—*Isospora amphiboluri.* Since almost all bearded dragons in captivity have coccidia, maybe the parasites are normal inhabitants. I have never seen data that evaluated the parasites of wild bearded dragons. Perhaps some of the first founding stock of bearded dragons brought into the U.S. were inadvertently exposed to coccidia. In any case, I take the stand that regardless of the source, coccidia should be eliminated whenever possible for the following reasons:

1) The parasites have a direct life cycle and build up to tremendous levels in captive animals. This is known as a superinfection.

2) Coccidia invade the intestinal lining cells to reproduce. In large numbers this can lead to gastrointestinal pain, diarrhea, malabsorption, and fluid loss. Eventually, this can lead to a failure to eat, weight loss, secondary nutritional disorders, and secondary bacterial infections.

3) Hatchling bearded dragons appear to pick up coccidia even when not exposed to the environment of the parent. This would infer transuterine or egg-related transfer. At some point we must break this cycle.

4) The coccidia may be transmissible to other reptiles. While coccidia are somewhat host specific, there have been no studies that I am aware of to determine whether *I. amphiboluri* affects other reptiles. I would be willing to bet that they do so quite readily.

So how do we get rid of coccidia? It's not easy, and it's not fun. Due to the lack of research on anticoccidial drugs for many decades, there are mainly two old standby sulfa drugs—sulfadimethoxine (Albon) and trimethoprim-sulfa (from many manufacturers). These drugs should be obtained from your reptile veterinarian only after a diagnosis of coccidiosis is confirmed with a fecal examination.

The protocol I use for eliminating coccidia was developed during an in-depth bar chat with two esteemed colleagues, Drs. John Rossi and Richard Funk. We shared information on treatments that, while reducing numbers, failed to eliminate all coccidia. We decided that using sulfa drugs resulted in the same outcome. I prefer giving oral sulfadimethoxine daily for three to five days, then every other day for as long as it takes. The secret to eliminating this disease resides in environmental control. You have to pretend that you are an obsessive/compulsive cage cleaner; and if you already are, then that's even better. To have a chance at breaking the exposure cycle with coccidia, the cage must be reduced to the bare essentials. Use newspaper or paper towels on the floor of the cage. Change the cage at least once or twice daily. Don't try to clean branches and rocks with cracks, crevices, or holes. Throw them out. Use cardboard cage furniture that you can eliminate daily. Water dishes should be simple and cleaned thoroughly twice every day.

Maintain the use of heat lamps and undercage heaters. Eliminate hot rocks and replace them with an undercage heater.

Feeder crickets, mealworms, wax worms, or veggies that are not eaten in a twenty-four-hour period should be *eliminated*. Do not recycle them or save them to use with other reptiles. Remember, the insects may have dined on the dragon droppings and would only serve to perpetuate the cycle.

Dr. Funk prefers having two side-by-side cage setups where one cage is always clean. Simply switch the bearded dragon to the other cage and clean the old one. Switch as often as necessary to decrease the possibility of exposure to fecal material and therefore coccidia oocysts. Sound like a pain? It is, because it has been my experience that it will often take up to six weeks for treatment to be successful. Even then, run a follow-up fecal exam two to three weeks after stopping the treatment protocol. Make sure your lizards are coccidia-free before mixing and matching dragons.

Treating a large group of bearded dragons in such a manner is obviously difficult, if not impossible. This regimen is a nuisance to practice for two lizards, much less two

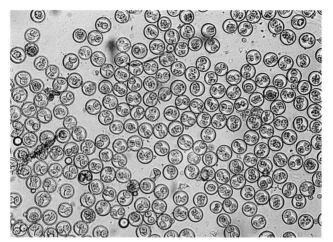

Note the hundreds of coccidial oocysts (100X) from a portion of bearded dragon stool.

hundred! I'm quite pessimistic that breeders with large numbers of dragons will take the steps required to eliminate their lizards' coccidia until more practical anticoccidial products are introduced. Not only would the lizards need to be separated as much as possible but outdoor enclosures would have to have dirt and other materials replaced. The good news is that once the group is clean they will stay that way unless new coccidia-bearing dragons are introduced. Studies are currently being conducted on new anticoccidial drugs for use in bearded dragons (with the cooperation of large dragon ranch operators such as Bob Mailloux at Sandfire Dragon Ranch), offering true hope that coccidia will someday be a thing of the past.

Remember the importance of quarantining new animals. I personally have seen dozens of coccidia-free groups of bearded dragons that were reinfected by the premature addition of a new arrival. New additions should be isolated for at least a few weeks and have fecals run on at least three samples over a period of weeks before being judged to be parasite-free.

A word of warning: Sulfa drugs should not be indiscriminately administered to every sick bearded dragon and should be used only if coccidia have been diagnosed. Sulfa drugs are potentially dangerous to dehydrated reptiles and need to be used under expert supervision. Rely on your

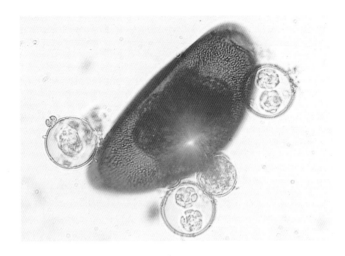

reptile veterinarian for diagnosis, prescription of medications, and performance of follow-up fecal examinations.

One last word about coccidia: I'd like to dispel the myth that coccidia oocysts are fragile. As a veterinary student, I was taught that oocysts are so fragile that it would be difficult to diagnose coccidia in some species due to the spontaneous decomposition of the thin-walled oocysts exposed to different drying and osmotic gradients. We should be so lucky! It has been my experience that oocysts can be found in petrified bearded dragon droppings, and they don't appear fragile in the least. I have placed various reptilian coccidial oocysts in 2–10 percent formalin to pickle them for later study, only to find out that some of the oocysts had continued their development! So clean your cages thoroughly with a soapy water/bleach solution (1 part bleach: 30 parts water). If the oocysts are not outright destroyed (the vast majority will be), then they will be removed mechanically.

Pinworms

Pinworms are another group of parasites that are ubiquitous in bearded dragons. While considerably less harmful than coccidia, pinworms can reach tremendous parasitic loads due to their direct life cycle.

While the treatment of pinworms is somewhat controversial (see, for example, Klingenberg, 1997) my feeling is that any parasite capable of creating superinfections should be eliminated. Pinworms are easily eliminated by administering oral fenbendazole (Panacur) daily for three to five doses, repeating this regimen again in ten days. Follow-up fecals should be checked three weeks after the last treatment.

Microsporidia

Dr. Elliott Jacobson recently reported the first cases of this intracellular protozoan parasite in three bearded dragons that had been inappetent and depressed, and that eventually succumbed to the protozoan parasites. While known to infect some amphibians and other reptiles, microsporidia had not been previously reported in bearded dragons.

These obligate intracellular unicellular protozoans are important pathogens of invertebrates and it was speculated that feeder insects were the source of infection, which is unlikely. The main source of transmission is probably spores shed from infected reptiles. While uncommon, this is a parasite that reptile veterinarians will be watching for in the future. It possesses characteristics that reptile owners and veterinarians dislike—a direct life cycle and resistant spores that can persist up to a year in the environment.

Tapeworms

While rarely diagnosed, I suspect that tapeworms are more common than is currently recognized. Tapeworms should be considered in bearded dragons that have been treated for coccidia and pinworms yet don't gain weight despite ravenous appetites,. An analogous situation was seen in ball pythons that had trouble gaining weight despite good appetites and appearing otherwise healthy. Occasionally these animals have been treated for tapeworms despite no definitive proof of their presence. Such a course of treatment should be based on discussions with a reptile veterinarian who knows the overall health parameters of the bearded dragon in question.

The most common means of diagnosing tapeworms is

The flat, white rice-shaped objects in this bearded dragon's stool are tapeworm proglottids.

by the presence of tapeworm segments (proglottids) in the feces. Proglottids are small, white, rice-shaped segments that can be found on the surface of the feces or moving away from it. These segments contain tapeworm eggs to be distributed to the environment either by desiccation of the segment (thereby releasing the eggs) or by being ingested. Tapeworm eggs can be found on routine fecal flotations but seem to be present only in very heavy infestations.

Treatment consists of either an oral or injectable dose of praziquantel (Droncit), which is repeated after two weeks. Tapeworms require intermediate hosts and have indirect life cycles, so self-exposure is not the problem it is with coccidia or pinworms.

Pentastomids

Dr. Charlie Innis was kind enough to send a fecal sample from an individual bearded dragon he was treating that was diagnosed with pentastomids. This was the only case I had heard of until running across a book on bearded dragons and frilled lizards written by Hauschild and Bosch (2000), which stated necropsies performed on ninety-three bearded dragons yielded eleven with pentastomids.

Pentastomids have an indirect life cycle, requiring intermediate hosts such as insects and rodents to complete their reproductive cycle. Extensive larval migration occurs before adults form in the lungs and complete the cycle by laying eggs that are then passed through the feces and into the environment. Despite large numbers and extensive larval migration of these prehistoric caterpillar-like parasites, most infestations occur without major symptoms. In some cases, there can be damage to the tissue during larval migration or when adults are in the lungs.

Treatment to date has been with high doses of ivermectin (Ivomec) which Dr. Innis has thus far found to reduce the number of ova passed but has not stopped the shedding altogether. His clinical trial wasn't completed at the time of this writing.

Pentastomids pose an unknown zoonotic risk and owners should be informed of this if their bearded dragons are affected. This is not a parasite I would take home to Mom.

External Parasites

Mites are not common, but when they do appear, they seem to be acquired from other reptiles within a collection. Mites do not appear to be indigenous to bearded dragons. Snake mites will infest bearded dragons and can be seen crawling on the lizards with the naked eye.

As with all mite infestations, treatment begins with the environment. At least temporarily, change the substrate to newspaper to eliminate hiding and breeding spots for the mites. Change the paper substrate at least two to three times a week. Reduce cage furniture to a minimum and eliminate all rocks or branches with cracks and crevices. An initial cage cleaning with a mix of water and bleach (one capful of bleach to each gallon of water) helps to mechanically eliminate mites and their eggs.

My preferred method of treating mites is to use an ivermectin-based spray (5–10 milligrams of ivermectin per quart of tap water). This solution is sprayed liberally in the cage after a thorough cleaning, with the lizard and water dish removed until the cage is dry. The lizard is gently but liberally sprayed, including the face and eyes, and returned to its dried cage. The water dish can be replaced once the cage and the lizard are thoroughly dried. This spray needs to be used every four to five days for three weeks.

Ivermectin is not a quick-kill product, so you may continue to see mites moving for the first few days of treatment. Store the spray in a dark cabinet between treatments and mix a new batch every thirty days.

For large, outdoor enclosures, I recommend removing the lizards to smaller indoor cages for individual treatment with the above ivermectin spray, while the outdoor enclosures are sprayed with a pyrethroid (type of insecticide) product designed for flea control in dogs and cats. The lizards should remain off the sprayed area until it has completely dried. If possible, it is ideal to keep the lizards in indoor cages while they are treated, but if they must be returned to the outdoor enclosures the lizards should remain off the sprayed areas until drying is complete. Most of the toxicity of pyrethroids has been linked to respiratory exposure in nonventilated containers, so a pyrethroid spray used as instructed in an open-air enclosure should be relatively safe. Pyrethroid has residual action and, depending on the product, need only be applied every one to three weeks. The dragon should be sprayed with the ivermectin product every four to five days for three weeks. Due to numerous hiding places and other variables, mites may be difficult to control in outdoor enclosures.

Nutritional Disorders in Bearded Dragons

One of the great benefits of being a reptile owner is that you get to observe feeding behaviors. Bearded dragons are just plain cool to feed. A healthy, hungry bearded dragon will perform an Olympic-quality floor exercise while polishing off a dozen crickets, mealworms, or wax worms. It is so much fun to feed insects to bearded dragons that sometimes that is all people feed them. As often as not, the dragons are so satisfied with their crickets that they refuse to eat vegetable matter. However MacMillen, Augee, and Ellis (1989) report that, in the wild, vegetable matter makes up as much as 90 percent and 50 percent of the diets for adult and juvenile bearded dragons, respectively.

There are benefits of having fresh veggies available daily:

❏ Greens and veggies are important sources of fiber, vitamins, and other nutrients.

❏ Availability of produce food reduces intraspecies mutilations.

❏ Crickets and other invertebrate prey can also gut load on the salad, prior to being eaten.

❏ Reducing the overall dietary protein and fat while increasing vegetable intake may extend longevity.

❏ Keep in mind though, that even when greens and veggies are fed along with crickets and other insects, nutritional disorders may occur.

Calcium Deficiency

The most common nutritional disorder I've seen in bearded dragons is calcium deficiency in the form of hypocalcemia (low blood calcium). The most common cause is a diet of almost exclusively crickets. Most feeder crickets come straight from a pet store and are not fed balanced diets (gut loaded) or dusted with nutritional supplements prior to being fed to dragons. Calcium deficiency is also seen in bearded dragons fed excessive amounts of meat products. These diets are low in calcium, and less calcium in the dragon's body leads to stimulation of receptors in the parathyroid gland, which in turn causes the release of parathyroid hormone (PTH). Increased levels of PTH activate cells in bone (osteoclasts) to start demineralizing bone to release calcium into the blood stream.

If the primary problem presents as soft bones and multiple fractures, the dragon's disease is termed metabolic bone disease (MBD). If the primary problem is twitching and seizures, then the dragon likely suffers from hypocalcemia (which is more common in juvenile dragons). Both forms are caused by too little calcium in the diet.

Vitamin D_3 Deficiency

The other main source of calcium deficiency I've seen in practice is vitamin D_3 deficiency or hypovitaminosis D. This fat-soluble vitamin is essential to the uptake and utilization of calcium in the body. Bearded dragons produce much of their vitamin D_3 from the reaction of UV light on their skin. This converts a cholesterol-derived product from pre–vitamin D to active vitamin D_3. The synthesis doesn't occur in dragons housed indoors without exposure to UV-B. (See the chapter on heating and lighting for information on UV-B, sunlight, and UV-B-emitting bulbs.)

Signs of Calcium Deficiency

Muscles require calcium to contract properly. Calcium deficiency leads to muscle pain and dysfunction such as when the smooth muscle of the gastrointestinal tract won't support peristaltic waves and results in constipation. Sometimes the first signs seen in young calcium-deficient dragons are bloating and constipation.

When the calcium level has been low for an extended period, muscle tremors set in. Toes and feet begin to twitch. This calls for immediate calcium supplementation.

As a bone is demineralized by the PTH-driven osteoclasts, the bony matrix is fortified with fibrous tissue (termed fibrous osteodystrophy), resulting in a brittle, swollen, and painful bone.

Calcium-deficient dragons initially look like any sick bearded dragon—weak, depressed, and reluctant to move. Very young dragons may be tremendously bloated and uncomfortable. Occasionally, twitching of toes and limbs is noted prior to handling. Sometimes twitching won't become evident until the lizard is stressed by handling. It has been my experience that hypocalcemic tetany, or twitching, appears in bearded dragons prior to extensive bony changes such as swollen limbs and softened jaws (rubber jaw). This is in contrast to green iguanas and other lizards, which may suffer extensive bony damage prior to muscle tetany.

Treatment

Bearded dragons with signs of calcium deficiency should be treated right away. Supplementation with calcium is ini-

tiated immediately. I prefer to use Neo-Calglucon, an oral product for humans, as my first source of calcium because it seems to be better absorbed than other products. Then review diet and husbandry to see if a vitamin D_3 injection is justified. Constipated animals are given gentle enemas or have their bowels emptied mechanically. Supportive care in the form of fluids and involuntary feeding is employed until a dragon is well enough to start eating its corrected diet. Some dragons are so weak that attempting oral calcium, fluids, or foodstuffs could easily result in aspiration pneumonia. Even the most debilitated lizard can have a pharyngostomy tube (placed by a qualified veterinarian), through which you can give medications, fluids, and food.

Prevention

As with most diseases, calcium deficiency is best prevented rather than treated. The reader should review the sections in this book on husbandry and diet. Certain strategies are emphasized here.

It is essential to expose young bearded dragons to a wide variety of vegetable matter so they get used to eating these foods and consume them as part of their usual diet. Some young bearded dragons enjoy vegetable human baby food into which small quantities of calcium can be stirred. For calcium supplementation, I suggest using calcium carbonate (no phosphorus or vitamin D_3), which can be

This juvenile bearded dragon was treated with Neo-Calglucon syrup, which led to excess residual syrup on its chin and predation by hungry crickets. Be aware that insect prey can become hunters instead of the hunted.

obtained from health food stores or can be purchased as Tums antacid tablets. I tend to dust veggies and/or crickets two or three times a week for young, growing dragons.

For provision of vitamin D_3, I employ two sources: a UV-B bulb and a powdered supplement. I place the bulb on the enclosure's screen top within 12 inches of the dragons and leave it on for twelve to fifteen hours in the summer and for ten to twelve hours in the spring and fall. I select the bulb carefully because only a few on the market produce significant levels of UV-B. I replace the bulb every six to nine months to ensure adequate UV-B production. In addition to the bulb, I use a powdered supplement that contains calcium and vitamin D_3, dusting it onto food no more than once every two weeks. Vitamin D toxicity is a real concern. It can easily be acquired through the use of products containing high levels of vitamin D_3 at every dusting. Calcium has one of the most narrow safety margins of all nutrients, and can produce signs of disease when fed in excessive amounts.

At this time, I'm not using a multivitamin product because I feed my dragons a broad range of veggies and gut-loaded insects that contain adequate nutrient content. If a multivitamin product is used with bearded dragons, it should be offered only once every two weeks. Use good food, supplements, UV bulbs, and common sense!

Force-feeding is very important in treating calcium-deficient dragons. Here a client uses a 1 cc syringe to feed her juvenile dragon a mixture of a vegetable-based baby food to which she has added a pinch of calcium carbonate powder and a little Pedialyte for fluids and electrolytes.

Adenoviruses in Bearded Dragons

Adenovirus disease in bearded dragons is poorly understood for the same reason most reptile diseases are poorly delineated—lack of funding for critical research. Here's what we do know.

Unfortunately, there are no specific signs to watch for in bearded dragons sick with adenovirus. Most of the bearded dragons that have been diagnosed with adenoviruses have had a history of failing to thrive, sometimes showing poor appetite, sometimes exhibiting diarrhea. Sometimes they die. The young, especially those four to twelve weeks old, appear to be affected more often than older specimens. Rather vague, wouldn't you say?

An affected animal is typically difficult to differentiate from one with coccidiosis or certain forms of calcium deficiency. To further complicate matters, dragons can have multiple disorders. A young bearded dragon with adenovirus could also have coccidiosis, which may or may not be causing problems at that moment. This young dragon could, or would, certainly develop nutritional disorders including hypocalcemia as poor food intake becomes a factor. These mix and match illnesses could go on and on, with one factor affecting another or making no difference. It's important to know if adenovirus is present in a sick dragon, but how do we accomplish this task?

The only method currently available to diagnose adeno-

This necropsied specimen with adenovirus illustrates a large liver that could have been accessed ante-mortem by a minor abdominal incision.

virus is autopsy. Most dead bearded dragons fail to demonstrate significant gross (readily visible) abnormalities of the internal organs. It is only on examination of tissues and cells with a microscope that the presence of intranuclear inclusions (material characteristic of certain viral infections), primarily in necrotic (dead) areas of the liver, is found. Such inclusions are *presumptive* evidence of adenovirus, but electron microscopy is required to *confirm* the diagnosis by demonstrating typical viral particles. This is *not* the same inclusion body disease that afflicts boids and pythons. Both are viral diseases but entirely different groups of viruses. The only similarity would be to make the suggestion that a liver biopsy is a useful diagnostic test, prior to the bearded dragon's death. While it may be somewhat risky to perform a surgical biopsy technique on a sick bearded dragon, the information obtained from liver biopsies is invaluable. A quick surgical biopsy on a living dragon is always preferable to a necropsy on a dead one.

While the technology exists to produce a simple blood test, this won't happen until it is demanded by you, the bearded dragon owner and veterinary client.

So do all bearded dragons exposed to adenoviruses die? No, some become chronic "poor doers" that come around slowly but can eventually recover, or at least appear to recover. Supportive care techniques—including force-feeding, fluids, and occasionally administrating antibiotics for secondary infections—increase their survival rate.

No one knows how long a bearded dragon that has recovered from adenoviruses carries and sheds the virus. And while we suspect the virus is given from one sick reptile to another through fecal and oral exposure, we truly don't have all the answers. So, whether you have a small group of pets or a large breeding colony, a virus severely complicates things. While there is always the risk of death, there is also the risk of spreading the disease by selling or trading the original lizards or their offspring. In essence, a diagnosis of adenovirus within a group of dragons should make them a closed group, with no additions or subtractions from the infected group. If future studies were to show that recovered lizards shed the virus for six weeks (this is hypothetical, not a fact!) and then fully recover, then an owner could quarantine an infected group for a reasonable time with hopes for the future. If studies reveal that infection and shedding is a lifelong phenomenon, then an owner would know that sick animals could never be moved from the group. This should clearly illustrate the need for basic research to answer such practical questions.

Other Health Concerns

Kidney Disease and Gout

Water is extremely important to the elimination of nitrogenous waste products in all reptiles. Because bearded dragons originate in the red sand deserts of Australia, it used to be assumed that bearded dragons have durable kidneys. Most desert-dwelling reptiles have adapted to extremely dry conditions by developing mechanisms to preserve water and to excrete concentrated uric acid. Apparently we haven't discovered or appreciated the methods employed by bearded dragons, because evidence of renal disease is on the rise.

Hauschild and Bosch (2000) stated that a group of necropsies on ninety-three bearded dragons revealed that 30 percent of the specimens had primary and secondary visceral gout. We need a very brief review of gout. As mentioned previously, the nitrogenous waste product that bearded dragons must eliminate from their blood stream is

Fluids are the most important initial treatment in cases of kidney failure. This bearded dragon is receiving an injection of fluids into the coelomic cavity.

uric acid, which is a highly insoluble product. If the kidneys become damaged by age, drugs, and chronic dehydration, they will be unable to properly filter out uric acid, which will increase in the bloodstream. If the resulting hyperuricemia becomes extreme, uric acid crystals are deposited into internal organs, causing severe inflammation and sometimes organ failure. The deposit of uric acid into tissues is often referred to as gout, and when this involves the internal organs it is called visceral gout. Deposition of uric acid due to kidney damage is termed primary visceral gout. If the kidneys are not damaged initially and dehydration leads to the hyperuricemia and deposits of uric acid, it is referred to as secondary visceral gout.

Visceral gout is usually fatal in bearded dragons unless corrected very early in its course. It is not yet known whether the visceral gout is primary (kidney damage) or secondary (dehydration). Some experts have speculated that wild bearded dragons retreat to moist underground burrows or stay buried to prevent loss of fluids. In the wild, adult bearded dragons appear to eat mainly vegetation, which can be a major source of moisture. Our hope is that husbandry factors such as excessively dry substrates, basking under a heat lamp, and a lack of moist veggies are the cause of dehydration, because these can easily be corrected.

Kidney failure due to excessive calcium and vitamin D_3

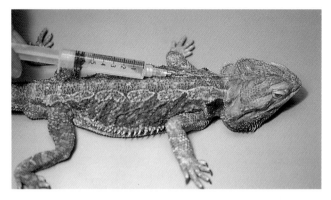

Mild dehydration should always be corrected in any sick dragon. A dehydrated dragon may receive a subcutaneous injection of fluids.

administration is common in other lizards, particularly the green iguana. The presence of excessive D_3 leads to the uptake of excessive calcium and subsequent mineralization of the kidneys. This syndrome hasn't been reported in bearded dragons, but it may just be a matter of time before we see it.

I hope further research on this topic will find some simple husbandry practices to help maintain captive specimens with normal kidneys. If diagnosed early, treatment centered around fluid therapy can be initiated and husbandry practices reviewed.

Prolapses

Prolapses are not common in bearded dragons, but they do occur, and should be treated as a relative emergency. The most common type seen in practice is hemipenal prolapse after breeding. The prolapsed hemipenes is a relatively large (3/4 inch long by 1/4 inch wide) bright red to dark red mass protruding from the vent of the affected male. The treatment is to *gently* clean and lubricate the tissue and then *gently* push it back into the vent with a lubricated Q-tip. The problem is that by the time this problem is noted, the tissue is often quite inflamed and swollen and cannot be replaced without it popping back out. If the tissue becomes excessively swollen, begins to dry out, or is traumatized by being dragged around the cage, the hemipenes' vascular supply could become damaged, necessitating an eventual amputation.

The abscess in the hemipenal region of this adult male bearded dragon was noted after the dragon had become lethargic and stopped eating. The source of the abscess is unknown, but it responded well to gentle debridement, topical antibiotic ointment, and a systemic antibiotic.

Due to the fact that so many variables exist with prolapses, the ideal course of action is to have your reptile veterinarian examine the dragon right away. The tissue can be evaluated for viability and sutured to help the hemipenes stay in place. Another important consideration is that some prolapses are of rectal tissue, which may be much more difficult to identify correctly. These prolapses are even more important to handle promptly and correctly. A bearded dragon can live without a hemipene, but it can't live without a functional rectum.

Rectal prolapses are often the result of chronic straining, so any dragon who is straining should be evaluated for parasites (such as coccidia, pinworms), gastrointestinal infections, constipation, gastrointestinal obstructions, and, in females, egg-binding. In addition, rectal prolapses can recur if their underlying cause is not identified and corrected.

Egg-Binding

Review the chapter on reproduction if there is any chance your female dragon could be gravid (or pregnant). A basic understanding of the bearded dragon reproductive cycle is helpful when dealing with problems. A gravid female is usually easy to detect, as her abdomen is swollen and her body weight increased. She looks pregnant. If the dragon is allowed to crawl across your open palm with your fingers

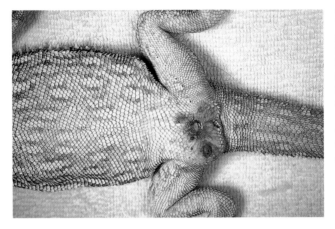

The cloacal abscess in this female adult bearded dragon may have resulted from a substrate made up of excessively abrasive rocks. Abrasions from "rub sores" became infected and weren't noticed until quite advanced.

slightly elevated, you can often feel the grape-sized eggs in her lower abdomen.

Behaviorally, pregnant dragons often continually dig and squat, move to a new spot and try again. They are agitated and tired, and usually won't eat properly due to both discomfort from the egg mass and the anxiety associated with egg-laying.

The easiest thing to try for an anxious lizard that appears ready to lay eggs and can't is to make sure the egg-laying site is appropriate. In the event that a bearded dragon is continuing to have problems, see a veterinarian right away. One of the most common problems is muscle weakness associated with subclinical calcium deficiency. The dragon's calcium isn't low enough for her to show other outward signs but is low enough to interfere with muscle contraction in her oviducts. Some dragons may be weakened by concurrent problems with parasitic, nutritional, viral, or bacterial diseases. This isn't a time to wait and see what happens without taking a great risk with the female's life. It is most important to make a diagnosis and try to correct so that eggs are laid successfully. In some cases, surgery might be necessary to save the female.

Respiratory Infections

When compared to other groups of lizards, members of the genus *Pogona* tend to be rather resistant to respiratory

The rectal prolapse in this bearded dragon was associated with an extremely heavy load of pinworms. Prolapses should be considered an emergency

infections. The most obvious symptoms of respiratory infections are gaping, forced exhalation of air, puffing of the throat, and a puffed-up appearance of the body. In severe cases, mucus will accumulate in the mouth and may emerge from the nostrils.

Remember that bearded dragons are desert dwellers. In mild respiratory infections, keep the animals at higher temperatures with daytime highs in the upper 80s to low 90s to allow immune system stimulation, enabling the lizard to fight off the infections. If the symptoms persist or worsen, take the animal to a reptile veterinarian for antibiotic therapy. De Vosjoli reports intermittent gaping behavior in heavily parasitized lizards and also in overheated bearded dragons. Respiratory disease is most often associated with subnormal temperatures.

Eye Problems

Veterinarians across the country have noted that bearded dragons are prone to developing swollen and runny eyes. A common hypothesis for this condition is that dust from sandy substrates is irritating, setting up an inflammatory conjunctivitis that is soon complicated by infections. This is somewhat puzzling as bearded dragons originate primarily from the red deserts of Australia where they are certainly exposed to a bit of sand. In any case, unprocessed silica sands and calcium-based sand products can certainly produce profound irritation if a few particles become trapped behind the third eyelid. Most of these problems respond nicely to a temporary change of substrate to newspaper for a couple of weeks while applying an artificial tears ointment or eye drop two to three times daily. The drops and ointment hydrate the eye and allow small particles to be flushed out.

Tail Rot

FAQ: *I now have had several bearded dragons whose tail tips have darkened. This eventually spread and part of the tail was lost. What causes this?*

The popular term for this kind of tail loss is tail rot. It is usually attributed to two causes. The first is trauma, such as an injury from nipping, or from being crushed or compressed by landscape materials. The other is accumulating tail tip sheds.

The first step should be to dip the damaged tail in a hydrogen peroxide solution as soon as it is noticed. This softens adhering shed skin, allows for its removal, and helps nip infection in the bud, so to speak. Dipping the tail in Betadine also works against infection and prevents the spread of tail rot. If this doesn't work, consider seeing a qualified reptile veterinarian. The best weapon against tail rot is prevention: keep babies segregated and well fed, making sure there are no landscape structures that can cause trauma to the tail, and soak bearded dragons in shallow water dishes to soften adhering shed skin.

In resistant cases, an ophthalmic antibiotic drop or ointment may be indicated for an infection. However, some veterinarians are reporting that some dragons still have eye problems, even with substrate changes and aggressive topical treatment. Other potential causes include allergic, nutritional, traumatic, or viral infections. I had one refractory case that did not go away until the animal was sedated and the inner layer of the third eyelid scraped, which suggests some type of foreign body was causing the problem.

Loss of Tail or Digits

Parts of tails and digits of juvenile bearded dragons are sometimes nipped off by cage mates. Unlike many other

Sandy substrates are often the cause of swollen and sore eyes. They respond to flushing with artificial tears. Difficult cases should be taken to a veterinarian.

lizard species, caudal autonomy, or the dropping of part of the tail is not part of the defensive repertoire of these species. Once lost, neither tail nor digits will grow back. Fortunately, infections seldom develop following these cannibalistic snacks.

Bearded Dragons: Are They Bullet-Proof?

Obviously they are not. However, bearded dragons are hardy lizards and in no way am I trying to discourage a potential owner from pursuing the opportunity to own and care for one or several dragons. My family's bearded dragon is the easiest lizard we've ever had. These lizards are extremely entertaining and gentle, one of the best lizards for hands-on activities.

Purchase your dragon from a reputable source. All new dragon owners should have their lizards examined by an experienced reptile veterinarian. At the very least you need to have fecal examinations performed—if your veterinarian doesn't suggest this then he or she is doing you a disservice. Eliminate any and all parasites. Quarantine (for parasites and viral diseases) any new bearded dragons for a minimum of two to three months. If you own a group of bearded dragons and one dies, refrigerate it until it can be necropsied by your reptile veterinarian.

I've covered the most common diseases of bearded

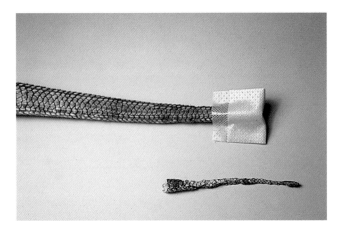

Unlike many other lizards, the tails of bearded dragons do not regrow after removal. The tip of this bearded dragon's tail was carelessly pinched in the lid of its cage.

This necropsied specimen died from visceral gout secondary to kidney failure that may have been initiated by sulfa drugs, which are generally safe but can cause renal damage. These kidneys are two to three times normal size because the body tried to compensate for increasing damage due to uric acid deposition.

dragons. Other diseases occur too, albeit less frequently. Dragons may also require surgery for such problems as broken bones, bite wounds, and placement of drains or feeding tubes. Today's dragons may receive CAT scans and laser surgeries, and may be examined with ultrasound and endoscopes. If your dragon becomes ill, find a veterinarian who enjoys dragons and is experienced in the medical and surgical care of reptiles.

The following health chart will help you determine whether your dragon needs veterinary care or other treatment for common symptoms.

Trouble Shooting Health Chart

Anatomical Region	Symptoms	Most common cause	Treatment
Eyes	Swollen and sore	Foreign bodies usually related to sandy substrates or calcium sand products	Flush with artificial tears or ointment. Use newspaper substrate until resolved. May need antibiotic ointment for secondary infections.
Nostrils	Occluded (plugged) with open-mouth breathing	Dried secretions from respiratory infections	Apply ointment twice daily until softened. A blunt probe may be required to mechanically remove the plug once softened. Observe for further signs of respiratory disease.
	Raw, swollen, or abraded nose	Rostral abrasion	Much less common than in other lizards. Caging should be evaluated for size, sharp edges, and availability of hiding spots. Mild abrasions can be treated with Neosporin or Polysporin.
Mouth	Mild distortion, hemorrhage, viscous secretions, or cheese-like pus. Excess salivation	Infectious stomatitis (mouth rot)	Unusual in bearded dragons and usually secondary to weakened oral tissues as seen with low calcium. Increase heat; offer a good basking gradient. Gently clean oral tissue with dilute Betadine, removing all loose and dead tissue. For all but the mildest cases, see veterinarian for antibiotics and to correct underlying conditions.
Throat	Distended or inflated; appears to bulge	Usually associated with respiratory infections	Increase heat (thermal gradient). If dragon is in respiratory distress, gently open mouth and attempt to make sure the mouth/throat is clear of debris. See veterinarian for all but mild cases.
Respiratory System (Glotttis/ trachea)	Gaping, open-mouth breathing, forced exhalation. Puffed appearance. Frothy and excessive saliva.	Respiratory infection. Intermittent gaping also seen with over-heating and threat behavior.	Increase heat (thermal gradient). If in respiratory distress, gently open mouth and attempt to make sure the mouth/throat is clear of debris. See veterinarian for all but the mildest cases to obtain systemic antibiotics, expectorants, drying agents, and nebulization, if needed.

Anatomical Region	Symptoms	Most common cause	Treatment
Neurological System	Depressed, decreased appetite, weak, normal behavior absent.	Signs of a sick bearded dragon but not specific	See reptile veterinarian to determine whether animal is affected by parasites, viruses, nutritional deficiencies, bacterial agents, etc. At the very least, a fecal examination needs to be performed. Don't miss your chance to get help.
	Head tilt, balance off, altered gait, flipping	Inner ear infections. Also seen with head trauma, overheating, bacterial meningitis, toxins and viruses.	Need veterinary exam as inner infections require systemic antibiotics and central nervous system disorders may require steroid anti-inflammatory drugs. An accurate diagnosis and aggressive supportive care are vital.
	Tremors, loss of body functions, spasms	Number of potential causes, including hypocalcemia (low calcium), hypoglycemia (low blood sugar), trauma, bacterial or viral infections, toxins etc.	Diagnosis is critical to differentiate low blood calcium from low blood sugar. Dragons that have low blood calcium have mild muscle tremors and twitching that is different from central nervous system origin seizures. Potentially life-threatening. Most common cause author has seen is low calcium levels in juvenile animals that responded well to treatment for hypocalcemia.
Skin	Excess dried skin with edges that are peeled up but will not come off	Retained shed	Bearded dragons are used to a dry environment and rarely have trouble. If lightly adhered, hold area underwater and gently rub skin off. If firmly adhered, do not force for fear of tearing skin. Add Tupperware hiding box with dampened sphagnum moss and wait for skin to loosen. Light misting of cage okay while shedding.
	Defined areas of dry, shrunken, adhered scales	Adhered secretions secondary to skin damage by mites and/or bacteria. Also possible burn form basking light.	Look carefully for mites. If found, refer to the External Parasite section. An antibacterial cream such as Silvadene (best), Neosporin, or Polysporin applied twice daily until lesion is resolved works best. Newspaper substrate is best whenever applying creams or ointments. See veterinarian for lesions that aren't resolving.

Anatomical Region	Symptoms	Most common cause	Treatment
Skin, Cont.	Abscesses, cysts	Firm granulomas (mass of inflamed granulation tissue, usually associated with infection), rarely tumors	See veterinarian for diagnosis. Needle biopsies are quick and easy. Treatment usually consists of surgical removal or lancing/debridement. Medications are dependent on cause. If abscesses are commonly encountered, move cage mate(s).
Body	Not gaining weight despite eating well. Behavior relatively normal.	Parasitism	Fecal examination is a must. If parasites are diagnosed, refer to section on treating parasites. It is difficult to eliminate coccidia but worth the effort. Treating the environment is as important as treating bearded dragons when dealing with parasites with a direct life cycle (i.e., coccidia or pinworms). There is possibility of pinworms, even if proglottids or eggs are not identified.
	Puffy, bloated appearance	Gravid (pregnant) females, respiratory infection	Pregnant females tend to appear and feel more plump when nearing egg-laying. Prepare cage for egg-laying. If accompanied by gaping, open-mouth breathing, forced exhalation, excessive salivation, etc., then a respiratory infection should be suspected. Refer to the respiratory section in this chart for treatment suggestions.

Trouble Shooting Health Chart

Anatomical Region	Symptoms	Most common cause	Treatment
Gastrointestinal	Puffy, bloated and painful straining to defecate. Tail swishing. Standing to avoid contact with abdomen.	Constipation, gastrointestinal foreign body	Adding vegetables to the diet may be all that is required to correct the problem. Fecal mass can often be palpated, and warm water enema might be required. Manipulation of colon under sedation might be necessary. Nonresolving cases or those that palpate a firm, cylindrical mass should have an X ray taken for a potential foreign body. Exploratory surgery may be indicated.
	Fetid, runny stools	Gastroenteritis, parasites	Fecal examination is a must. A fecal culture may be required if diarrhea doesn't respond to antibiotic treatment.
	Weight loss, weakness, poor appetite	Parasites	Fecal examination is a must and if parasites are diagnosed, read section on treating parasites.
Muscular/ skeletal	Reluctance to move, swollen and painful legs, distorted or kinked tail, soft jaw	Metabolic bone disease (MBD), calcium deficiency	Calcium deficiency may result from either lack of calcium in diet, being fed excessive phosphorus, or a lack of vitamin D_3. Very mild cases will respond to a corrected diet and calcium supplementation. Bearded dragons in pain and are reluctant to eat should be seen for calcium injections and vitamin D_3 (if indicated by dietary history). Refer to the chapter on nutrition.
	Fused, distorted vertebrae	Sequelae (pathological conditions that result from disease) to MBD	During episodes of calcium deficiency, bone may be broken down, leading to more brittle and weaker bones, leading to pathological fractures. If calcium becomes available, these previously weak and fractured areas become overmineralized to compensate and form bony lumps.

CHAPTER 11:

FRILLED DRAGONS: THEIR CARE AND BREEDING

by Jerry Cole

The frilled dragon (*Chlamydosaurus kingii* Grey 1825) is another Australian agamid that has attracted the attention of bearded dragon hobbyists. Large size, unusual appearance, and a docile temperament make a frilled dragon an interesting candidate if you are considering adding another type of "dragon" to your collection.

For many years, ever since the ban of reptile exports by Australia in the late 1960s, frilled dragons were lizards that most people only knew from photographs and that herpetoculturists only dreamed of owning. I saw my first frilled dragons in a popular TV advertisement in the early 1980s, while living in Japan. The flared frill, open-mouth display and ungainly bipedal running greatly amused the Japanese, sending them into fits of laughter. Although a few specimens had been offered on U.S. dealers' lists in the 1980s, it wasn't until 1993, with the first Indonesian exports, that these odd lizards became readily available to hobbyists in the U.S. and the U.K. This allowed hobbyists to develop the methods for keeping and breeding this species with regularity, setting the groundwork for establishing it in the hobby.

The distribution of frilled dragons is restricted to Northern Australia and Southern New Guinea, where they

This frilled dragon performed a sudden bipedal leap and frilled display when photographed.

The Indonesian frilled dragon is the most readily available morph in the hobby. Photo by Jerry Cole

inhabit dry forests and savannahs. Most specimens in captivity are from Irian Jaya, the western half of New Guinea. The specimens in my possession supposedly came from the Merauke region of New Guinea. There are also a small number of frilled dragons of Australian origin established and bred in the herpetocultural hobby. The most impressive forms are said to originate from Australia's Northern Territories. These frilled dragons tend to be larger and more colorful than Indonesian animals, with adult males also developing characteristic white cheek areas. Both Indonesian and Australian forms, as well as hybrids, are currently bred in captivity.

Appearance

Frilled dragons are medium to large lizards in the family Agamidae. The average sizes and weights of the Indonesian form common in the hobby are as follows:

Males: Snout to vent is 8 inches; total length is 26 inches; average weight is about 14 ounces (400 grams).

Females: Snout to vent is 7 inches; total length is 18 inches; average weight is about 5 ounces (150 grams).

Northern Australian animals can reach a length of 36 inches and more than twice the average weight of Indonesian animals.

Frilled lizards are slender, generally mostly gray or brown with yellow and white, with varying amounts of orange or red on their frills. When threatened and during courtship these lizards open their mouths wide to extend the folded frill. It flares into a flattened disc 8–9 inches across in Indonesian animals and up to a foot across in large Australian males. The yellow inside of the open mouth contrasts sharply with the surrounding frill. If caught in the open, the frill may be displayed from a raised bipedal stance while facing the source of threat. This is a glorious display unlike anything performed by any other species of lizard. The frill is folded back against the neck and body, when it's not in use. Because its expansion is linked to the actions of the mouth (the muscles that erect the frill are connected to the hyoid bone), the folded frill flutters when frilled dragons eat and drink.

Sexing

As you can see from the size data, adult frilled dragons are relatively easy to sex on the basis of size differences. Hatchlings and juveniles are difficult to accurately sex, although as they grow older, males develop significantly larger frills (extending further down the back and front when folded) and slightly enlarged jowls. Another method for sexing is manual eversion of the hemipenes. This consists of lifting anal scales to expose the vent and using a back-to-front rolling motion of the thumb, applying pressure from the tail-base toward the vent to force the

hemipenes to protrude. This method requires care and experience, but it has proven effective for sexing subadults of this species. Because of the risks of causing injury this method is not recommended with hatchlings and juveniles.

This large, colorful male "red phase" morph (displaying to its owner) originates from Australia's Northern Territory.

Longevity

Frilled lizards are relatively long-lived lizards. A male obtained as an adult lived for nine years and eleven months (Slavens and Slavens, 1996, 2000), and there are currently several living imported adults that have been in captivity for at least eight years. Adjusting for age to maturity, this suggests that this species could achieve a life span of twelve or more years.

Before Buying a Frilled Lizard

Few lizards are more endearing than baby frilled dragons. Given regular attention that includes hand-feeding (king mealworms are particularly suitable for this purpose), frilled dragons tend to become quite tame and, in the case of males, may develop a high level of responsiveness. Only after you have seen a male frilled dragon running, body raised on its hind legs, across a room to come grab food can you fully appreciate how endearing these gangly lizards can be. However, as much as frilled dragons have many of the best qualities one could expect from a pet lizard, the fact remains that these large lizards require sizeable enclosures (five or more feet in length) as well as a minimum of heat and light sources. Frilled dragons also consume large amounts of insects and occasional vertebrate prey. Prospective owners must carefully consider these requirements.

Selecting a Frilled Dragon

When frilled lizards were first imported in the early 1990s, they fetched a high price, ranging from $600 to $1000 each. Fortunately, they proved to be a relatively hardy species, and now both imports and captive-bred babies are available at a fraction of their original price. Considering the risks and problems of establishing imported "frillies," captive-bred frilled dragons should always be your first choice. Wild-collected specimens are generally heavily parasitized and many harbor mites, most readily seen in the back folds of the frills. If you choose a wild dragon, have a qualified veterinarian perform a fecal examination and treat accordingly. Spraying the mite-infested area with a solution of ivermectin usually proves effective in getting rid of these pests.

Always chose specimens with good body weight, notably around the pelvic area where the first signs of weight loss tend to become apparent. The specimens should have bright, clear eyes and an alert posture, bearing in mind that one of their defense mechanisms is to freeze and flatten themselves down when they perceive a threat. The snout and the area around the mouth should be examined for injuries or swellings. The limbs should be equal in proportion with no asymmetrical swellings, particularly at the wrists and ankles. Finally, ask to hold the lizard. It should not feel limp in your hand. The head should not hang down. Turn it around and examine the

belly area. Look for red patches on the skin, which can be a telltale sign of bacterial infection. Next, examine the vent and cloacal area. The anal scales should appear flush with the body. The vent should be free of smeared fecal matter, swelling, and scabs. When you handle and examine these lizards, don't forget about the two fanglike teeth at the front of their jaws. Don't get bitten.

Australian male frilled dragon in full display

Frill Displays

As babies, these lizards are very prone to threatening you with mouth and frill open wide. However, in time, most frilled lizards lose this aggressiveness and tend to become very placid animals. Once settled in captivity, they rarely display an open frill except under extreme provocation. Once habituated to the human environment, these lizards can nonetheless still be tricked into displaying an expanded frill for the purpose of putting on a show or taking photographs of a frilled dragon in full display. Techniques such as suddenly confronting them with a mirror, a quickly opened umbrella, a camera flash, a twirling lightbulb, a snake, a large lizard, or a dog have proven successful in eliciting a frilled display.

You can use cork rounds and slabs to increase activity areas for these arboreal lizards. Photo by Jerry Cole

Enclosures

Frilled Dragons are adapted for an arboreal life, and their resting posture consists of sitting in a vertical position with the head raised. To accommodate this behavior, a large and tall cage is a must. The floor surface of the cage enclosure should obviously be determined by how many lizards you plan to keep. As a general rule, I suggest giving them as large an enclosure as you can provide. We successfully reared, maintained, and bred two male and three female frilled dragons in a 66-inch-long x 48-inch-high x 24-inch-wide cage for five years. Solid-walled enclosures with glass fronts and screen tops are ideal because they allow viewing, help increase relative humidity, and reduce the risks of snout abrasion.

As to furnishing the cage, we have found that the best substrate for these lizards seems to be bark chips, (a number of people using sand have experienced toe infections, which resulted in the loss of toes). To provide climbing areas, we add long cork bark tubes running from floor to ceiling. We also line the walls of the cages with cork bark tiles. These rough tiles, which frilled dragons can readily climb, can effectively quadruple the useable space available for the animals and enable the more nervous or subdominant individuals a better chance to avoid the more domi-

nant ones. The cage should be maintained at approximate-ly 75–85°F ambient temperature with a basking site heated by a spotlight that reaches 90–95°F. A reptile UV-B generating light should be used (ZooMed Repti-Sun 5.0 or similar UV bulbs). Fresh water should always be available.

Female "red phase" frilled dragon

Gender and Number

Unless you intend to breed your frilled dragon, you will likely find that males tend to be more interactive and lively as single pets. They also grow larger and have more colorful frills than females have. Many keepers have reported that males are generally more outgoing and display a greater degree of responsiveness than females, who tend to be shy and more likely to adopt cryptic behaviors.

Although we have had good success keeping two males and several females in the same enclosure, other breeders have reported better success housing only a single male per enclosure with multiple females. Because male frilled dragons are territorial and tend to form a dominance hierarchy when several are kept together, subdominant males may become stressed and start declining. Closely observing your animals' behaviors should allow you to determine their compatibility.

Feeding and Watering

Frilled lizards are voracious feeders and rarely present problems. We offer a variety of the following: House crickets (*Acheta domestica*), field crickets (*Gryllus bimaculatus*), locusts (*Schistocerca gregaria*), giant mealworms (*Zophobas morio*), and appropriate-sized rodents (the length of the prey body is equal or less than the head length of the lizard), are all easily available from specialist pet stores or national mail-order companies. The only times that I have ever seen my frilled dragons eat vegetation is when I have placed fresh cork-bark tubes in their cage. The dragons pick and eat the dried mosses and lichens growing on the cork bark. Chris Estep, owner of Reptile Haven, has reported that his captive-raised frilled lizards have learned to feed on watermelon offered as a treat.

We feed juvenile frilled lizards daily on small crickets (head width is a good criterion for prey size selection), dusted with a vitamin-mineral powder every other day, and with the occasional wax worm (*Galleria mellonella*) offered as a treat. Once they have grown to 6 inches in total length (approximately 50–100 percent of their original hatching size) we give them a pink mouse once a week and only offer crickets every other day. When they reach about 8–10 inches total length, we also start feeding them giant mealworms and medium-sized locusts. This regime continues into maturity, with the only adjustment being the size of prey, which varies according to the lizard's size.

We provide water in large shallow pans. To assure that these lizards get enough water and to increase relative humidity, we spray the animals once daily until we observe them drinking from the water bowl.

Breeding

Assuming you have both sexes in good condition, initiating breeding is not difficult. Under our husbandry regime, captive-bred and -raised frilled dragons reach sexual maturity at fifteen to eighteen months of age. To achieve successful breeding, usually you have to cycle them by manipulating several environmental factors. In the wild, frilled dragons live in dry forests and savannahs that have distinct seasons—typically long dry seasons alternated by shorter rainy seasons. To initiate breeding, simply simulate a distinct dry season followed by a rainy season.

We have consistently had good results with the following procedures. When females are in good condition we switch off their basking spotlight, which effectively drops the cage's ambient temperature to 70–80°F. We also reduce the photoperiod (day length) from sixteen to twelve hours a day and stop spraying their cage. This is continued for six to eight weeks, during which time activity levels and food and water intake decrease dramatically. In the wild, this would correspond with the dry season, a period when these lizards retreat to the uppermost branches of their trees and effectively estivate. After this two-month rest period, the regular husbandry regime is resumed. Spotlights are turned on for fourteen or more hours a day, temperature is raised back to normal, and heavy spraying with water is performed once or twice a day. As a result, food and water intake increase dramatically.

Normally, within ten to fourteen days of a return to a rainy season (or normal) regime, the dominant male lightens in color, with the end third of the tail darkening. The male also starts becomes agitated and irritable. At this time he chooses the best vantage point in the cage to survey his territory, constantly head-bobbing, frilling, swishing his tail like an angry cat does, and rushing around the cage to assert his dominance on all cage mates. Females submit by lowering their bodies and moving their heads in a side-to-side circular movement. More rarely, they arm-wave as a submissive behavior. Like juvenile bearded dragons, frilled dragons often perform arm-waving when young and cease to do so as they grow older.

Mating is a brief procedure, a short chase during which the male bites hold of the female's frill behind the head and pins her to the ground. Then, with his back leg, he performs scratching motions until he can lift the female's back leg and bring their vents together. Actual mating is brief and only takes one to five minutes.

As a nest box, we offer female frilled dragons a tray that is 24 inches long x 15 inches wide and about 7 inches deep, with damp peat as a laying medium. When gravid females become obviously distended and their bodies appear almost pear shaped, they begin to look for a site to lay eggs. This process, which usually lasts up to two weeks before laying, consists of short burrow-digging sessions. Few problems are associated with egg-laying as long as there is a suitable laying site and the females are left undisturbed. Under our conditions, most eggs are laid in late morning or early afternoon, taking approximately one to two hours to lay. Most of the clutches laid in our facilities consist of six or seven eggs with the largest being nine. However, the larger Northern Australian frilled dragons are reported to commonly lay single clutches of twelve or more eggs with one record of a female laying twenty-three eggs (Bedford, Christian, and Griffiths 1993).

After laying, the female then covers her eggs. Interestingly, for up to twenty-four hours after laying (if the eggs are left in the nest), any disturbance to the nest area may evoke interest from the female and will lead her to tidy up again.

Incubation

Eggs should be removed at the first opportunity anytime after laying is completed and placed in a ventilated plastic storage container filled with 2 inches of lightly dampened vermiculite. Bury the eggs on their sides in the incubating medium so that two-thirds of each egg remains exposed. Then place the container into an incubator set at 83–85°F. Hatching occurs between eighty and ninety days (this is also about the period required for our females to lay the next clutch—one clutch in, one clutch out!).

Although some breeders have recommended higher incubation temperatures, others have indicated that high temperatures can lead to delayed development and a high rate of embryo death (pers. comm. Bob Mailloux; and Weis 1996). Those who successfully hatch frilled dragons using incubation temperatures that exceeds 85°F usually allow significant day/night fluctuations with night drops into the upper 70s (°F). There was a study in which they measured the ground temperature of the nests of Northern Territory frilled dragons and obtained average measurements (midmorning/late afternoon) of 85°F and 89°F (Bedford, Christian, and Griffiths 1993). These data suggest the possibility that there could be variations in incubation tolerances between the different forms, that is, between Indonesian and Australian frilled dragons. There is also evidence that in frilled dragons, incubation temper-

Baby frilled dragons are hatching from eggs half-buried in moistened vermiculite. Photo by Jerry Cole

ature may determine sex. A preponderance of males in the many clutches we have hatched at 85–86°F supports the possibility of temperature-dependent sex determination. Others have reported higher female ratios if the eggs are incubated at 82–83°F. Clearly this information suggests the subject of incubation in this species warrants further investigation

After the egg are slit, frilled babies stay inside the shell for up to twenty-four hours before emerging. They should never be disturbed during this period. Once out, they enter a stage in which they lie still and look like they are dead for another twenty-four hours. Although they don't do much during this period, the hatchlings are still fun to watch. Baby frilled lizards are among the most endearing young reptiles, with high-contrast patterns that are far crisper and bolder than on adults.

Reproductive Rate

In the wild, I believe frilled dragons probably lay one to three clutches of eggs annually, depending on a combination of factors including availability of food and water and climatic conditions. In captivity, if conditions are right, they can dramatically exceed this rate. Our F1 (first generation captive-bred) frillies of early 1995 were cycled in mid-1996. Two females then started to lay a clutch of eggs every eighty to ninety days and did not stop until October 1999, even when subjected to a simulated dry season. The fertility of the many clutches was 100 percent.

To help females survive this kind of intensive breeding, be sure to provide ample amounts of high-quality food. The importance of caring for fertile females becomes particularly evident once you consider that a clutch of eggs can represent 20–30 percent of a female's body weight. Captive female frilled dragons have such a strong drive to reproduce that it can override their ability to sustain themselves. Only heavy feeding can allow a female to regain enough weight to allow her to lay again three to ten weeks later and remain healthy.

Diseases

Once established, frilled dragons are generally a hardy lot; even imports may live many years with few health problems. However, among imports, parasites are a common problem that must be diagnosed and treated. Additionally, adult imports can initially be restless, and if kept in too small or abrasive enclosures such as wire mesh, they may damage their snouts. This is best prevented by providing the right type of enclosure with cork tubes, angled branches, or small trees to give these animals a sense of security and the opportunity to hide from view.

Captive-bred specimens, although usually better acclimated, are not necessarily problem-free. Possibly because many breeders of frilled dragons also work with bearded dragons, both pinworms and coccidiosis (the bane of bearded dragon breeders) have been reported in captive-bred frilled dragons. As a rule, an animal that fails to gain or maintain weight should always be checked for parasites by a qualified reptile veterinarian. In babies, as with most other insect-eating lizards, metabolic bone disease (soft bones leading to deformities, inability to feed and/or move) caused by inadequate availability of calcium is of special concern. Prevent this disease by providing a high-quality diet supplemented with a vitamin/mineral supplement and a UV-B light source. Frilled lizards also risk damage to the frill from trauma or tearing. Shedding problems also sometimes occur when these lizards are kept too dry, at a low relative humidity, and without regular misting. In older animals, gout, apparent as hard swellings of the ankle or wrist areas, has been reported with some frequency. Suspected causes of this disorder include inadequate hydration, or feeding animals kept at suboptimal temperatures.

Old Age

It is only recently that some attention has been brought to reptile geriatrics, notably by reptile veterinarian John Rossi (Rossi and Rossi 1996) and more recently by de Vosjoli, Donoghue, and Klingenberg (1999). The latter presented an ontogenetic framework (called life stages) as a basis for adjusting husbandry practices.

How does one care for old frilled dragons? If they are sick and requiring labor-intensive and costly care, the reasonable thing to do is to opt for humane euthanasia. On the other hand, many of the larger lizards, like people, seem to simply get old and require a little extra care. Because many old lizards have been long-term responsive pets—almost members of the family—it is natural for attached owners to want to provide supportive care in the last stages of their lives.

Some of the ailments of old frilled lizards include opacities of the lens that can result in partial blindness, decreased activity, and gout. Eventually this disabled stage leads to an extended period of inactivity that can last several weeks, sometimes months, prior to death. Supportive help during these senior and terminal stages usually means hand-watering, bringing food within easy reach, or even hand-feeding, and maybe even helping an aging, disabled frillie to move in and out of the sun.

WORKS CITED AND RECOMMENDED READING

Bartholomew, G. A. and V. A. Tucker. 1963. Control of Changes in body temperature, metabolism, and circulation by the agamid lizard, *Amphibolurus barbatus*. *Physiological Zoology* 36:199–218.

Bedford, G. S., K. A. Christian, and A. D. Griffiths. 1993. Preliminary Investigations on the Reproduction of the Frillneck Lizard (*Chlamydosarus kingii*) in the Northern Territory. In Lunney, D., and D. Ayers. *Herpetology in Australia*. Transactions of the Royal Zoological Society of New South Wales, 414 s. c. kingii.

De Vosjoli, P., S. Donoghue, and R. Klingenberg. 1999. The Multifactorial Model of Herpetoculture. Part 1: Ontogeny. *The Vivarium.* 11:1.

Hauschild, A. and H. Bosch. 2000. *Bearded Dragons and Frilled Lizards*. Matthias Schmidt Publications. Germany. *Highly recommended for anyone interested in these species and has an extensive bibliography.*

Klingenberg, R. 1993. *Understanding Reptile Parasites*. Irvine, Calif.: Advanced Vivarium Systems.

Klingenberg, R. 1997. Pinworms: Friend or Foe. *The Vivarium.* 8:5, 23–24.

MacMillen, R. E., M. L. Augee, and B. A. Ellis. 1989. Thermal Ecology and Diet of Some Xerophilous Lizards from Western South Wales. *Journal of Arid Environments* 16:193–201. *This is the often-quoted reference on the predominantly plant diet of adult bearded dragons. Also contains valuable information on thermoregulation.*

Rossi, J. and R. Rossi. 1996. *What's Wrong with My Snake?* Irvine, Calif.: Advanced Vivarium Systems. 61–64.

Slavens, F. and K. Slavens. 1996, 2000. Reptiles and Amphibians in Captivity. Breeding-Longevity. Seattle, Wash.: Slaveware.

Weis, P. 1996. Husbandry and Breeding of the Frilled Lizard in *Advances in Herpetoculture*. *International Herpetological Symposium.* 1:87–92.

INDEX

40–42, 48–49, 92–93

AUTHOR BIOGRAPHIES

Philippe de Vosjoli an expert on reptile husbandry who revolutionized herpetoculture with the publication of *The Vivarium* magazine and the Advanced Vivarium Systems line of books. With over a million books in print, he is the best-selling author of more than twenty books and 100 articles on the care and breeding of amphibians and reptiles. With Robert Mailloux, he pioneered the commercial breeding of bearded dragons and coauthored the best-selling *General Care and Maintenance of Bearded Dragons*, Amazon.com's # 1 book on reptile care in 1998.

Robert Mailloux is the owner of Sandfire Dragon Ranch and was responsible for developing the commercial breeding of bearded dragons in the United States. He is the originator of the spectacular Sandfire morph of the bearded dragon. He is an amphibian specialist and was the first person to commercially breed several of the frog species now readily available in the pet trade. With Philippe de Vosjoli, he has coauthored several articles and books on the herpetoculture of bearded dragons and tropical frogs.

Susan Donoghue, V.M.D., has combined a life-long love of herps with her professional training as a board-certified diplomate in the American College of Veterinary Nutrition. She has written more than fifty publications in peer-reviewed scientific journals and more than one-hundred chapters and articles on nutrition and health. She has served as editor for several publications and as president of the American Academy of Veterinary Nutrition. She owns Nutrition Support Services, Inc., designs and markets the Walkabout Farm line of dietary products for herps, and is an avid breeder of bearded dragons.

Roger Klingenberg, D.V.M.'s, life-long passion for reptiles inspired his pursuit of a veterinary degree from Colorado State University. His combined skills of veterinary specialization in treating reptiles, along with over thirty years of experience keeping and breeding a variety of lizards, snakes and turtles, have helped bring him to the forefront of reptile veterinary medicine and surgery. He has shared his extensive knowledge and experience through lectures, magazine articles, textbook chapters, and scientific papers. He is the author of *Understanding Reptile Parasites* and coauthor of several best-selling books on reptile care including *The Box Turtle Manual, The Ball Python Manual,* and *The Boa Constrictor Manual.*

Jerry Cole is an experienced herpetoculturist who has kept and bred reptiles since the early 1980s. In 1984, he and his wife Belinda formed B.J. Herp Supplies, which they are still running today. Over the years they have developed many new reptile-oriented products, the best known probably being Natures Image T-shirts. Their business is currently run from purpose-built facilities on their Farm in South West England and supplies captive-bred livestock, equipment, literature, etc. to pet stores and hobbyists throughout Europe.

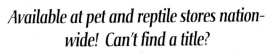